CLASS BACKWARDS

*Growing up in Nordeast Minneapolis
in the '40s and '50s*

By Edison Authors

©2012 Edison Authors

Printed in the United States of America

All rights reserved. No part of this book may be reproduced or transmitted in any form, or by any means, electronic or mechanical, including photocopy, recording, or any other information storage and retrieval system without permission in writing from the Edison Authors committee..

Selected photos in this book have appeared with the permission and through the courtesy of:

The Hennepin County Library, Special Collections

The Minnesota Historical Society

Publisher:

Edison Community and Sports Foundation A 501(c)(3) organization

CLASS BACKWARDS

Growing up in Nordeast Minneapolis in the '40s and '50s

Dedication: To all those willing to carry on the traditions of a peaceful coexistence in Nordeast.

"Wrinkles should merely indicate where smiles have been"- Mark Twain

Acknowledgments

The Edison Authors Committee would like to thank first our families and friends for putting up with us for these three years as we hammered this book together. We'd also like to thank all of the community of authors that put up with our nagging to send in more material. Then, of course, there are our friends and acquaintances who have specific technical skills who've come to the forefront and bailed us out when we got in over our heads technically.

Robert Anderson has provided invaluable help as we've worked out our illustrations. Norman and Judith Larson have performed yeoman's tasks as they have proofed and re-proofed our copy.

Credits:

Covers by Cathy Kohout
Photo restoration, photo collages, and chapter layout by Larry Kohout
Illustrations by Ian and Rochelle Cunningham, Cathy Kohout, Richard Myslajek,
   Rod Nelson, and Norm Solberg
Original photos by Rodney Nelson
Co-Editors- Carol Larson and Rod Nelson
   Assistant Copy Editors - Norman and Judith Larson

Content

FRONT MATTER
    Title Page i
    Copy Right and Publication data ii
    Dedication iii
    Acknowledgements & Credits v
    Content vii
    Preface x

INTRODUCTION 1

CHAPTER 1: WHERE IN THE WORLD IS NORDEAST 3
    Nordeast is Beautiful 7

CHAPTER 2: LESSONS FROM THE PAST 9
    Depression 9
    How We Handled the Depression 12
    World Wars I & II 14
    The significance of War 20
    The End of War 21

CHAPTER 3: OUR HERITAGE—GRANDMA WORE A BABUSHKA 23
    Making It In a New Country 27
    Poland 29
    A Menu of Memories 31

CHAPTER 4: ALL THIS AND HEAVEN TOO 35
    Get Me To The Church On Time 38
    The Young and The Restless 41
    Discovering Differences 42
    Growing Up Under the Influence 46
    Dead People 54
    Weren't All Weddings Polish? Oom Pa Pa Oom Pa Pa 59
    Final Writes 61

CHAPTER 6: HAPPY DAZE 79
    Our Homes Inside and Out 79
    Little Things That Made a House a Home 85
    Gardens 88
    Food Glorious Food 90
    Neighborhood Markets 93
    Home Deliveries 105
    Meal Times 108
    Chores 109

CHAPTER 7: CAN JOHNNY COME OUT AND PLAY 113
    Games We Played On Our Own 114
    Places to Play 117
    Winter Sports 124
    Summer Sports 130
    Family Life and Inventive Games 137

CHAPTER 8: THAT'S ENTERTAINMENT 145
    The Movies 146
    Television 157
    Don't Forget the Telephone 160
    Band-Choir Concerts 161
    Top Ten Dumb Things We Thought Would Be Entertaining 164

CHAPTER 9: GRADE SCHOOLS 171
    Pillsbury 172
    Edith Cavell 176
    Thomas Lowry 177
    Sheridan 179
    Pierce, Webster, and Prescott 183
    Digging Deeper—School Memories K-6 190

CHAPTER 10: GETTIN' AROUND 197
    Street Cars 198
    Train Travel 205
    Trips Outside the City 212

CHAPTER 11: THE BEGINNING OF A NEW ERA: THE EARLY '50s 221
    Some Backward Thoughts 222
    And We Became Aware 229
    Lasting Pictures of the past 239
    Our First Crushes 240
    Our Fondest Memories 243

BACK MATTER 251
    List of Authors 251
    List of Illustrations 252

Preface

Three years ago, a group of us from Edison, class of '58, decided to write and solicit recollections from our classmates—what it was like to grow up in Nordeast Minneapolis in the '40s and '50s. Surprisingly, 54 people responded.

Our intentions were to record those things that each of us remembered as we remembered them. Not to record history. You will find conflicting information within the book. That simply indicates the various authors' differing recollections. It also demonstrates how difficult it is to get really accurate history when you are only half a century away from the happenings. Gathering all these recollections has been time consuming and in some cases frustrating, but we, the committee, have found it a very entertaining look at the middle of the 20th century. So enjoy our recollections. Where you find differences, you will have to determine for yourself whose version is more accurate. Or simply read for the fun of it.

There was another side to this: it also brought us back in touch with our classmates and memories long since forgotten. It has resulted in a book, that will be a keepsake. These pages are a nostalgic look at an era, reflecting pride in our heritage, our families and the times we shared.

THE EDISON AUTHORS' COMMITTEE

INTRODUCTION

This book is for anyone who is intrigued looking at their lives and realizing how their upbringing has affected them. All stories are first-hand recollections of our place and time in history. Hopefully, like we did, you may pause, reflect, and have a quick laugh, jarring loose memories of days long since forgotten.

We came to our 50th class reunion sporting wrinkles and somewhat altered in appearance since our high school days at Edison. We'd grown older, that's a fact. But as we looked around the room or joined a group, a strange thing happened. Everyone changed into the kids we once knew: the pals from long ago, the ones who made our hearts flutter, kids from our neighborhood. It didn't take very long to go back in time before we started with our stories: Remember the time when we…? and who was that family who lived down the street?

CLASS BACKWARDS — INTRODUCTION

Red, Bev, and Carol Lyons

Sharon Matt on her mother's lap

The years seemed to disappear. We entertained each other with what we remembered from our past.

Something else emerged from these conversations however: we realized we grew up in an era that will never come again, in a part of Minneapolis with a unique history. These stories were good. We reasoned, if we didn't collect what we could and write them down, who else would preserve them?

After all, we lived it. It's taken more than a year to put them all together but we believe this is truly a keepsake. Looking backward, in our own way, we had a lot of class.

Nordeast corner of Edison High School

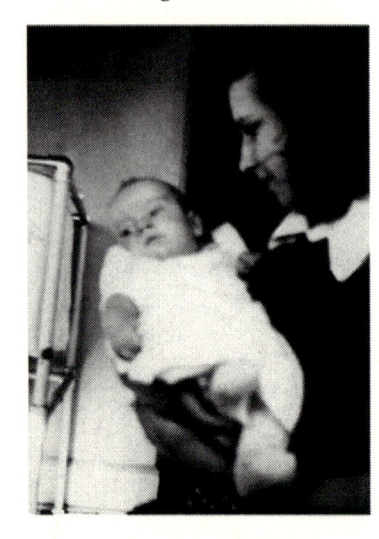

Rod Nelson in his mother's arms

CHAPTER ONE:
WHERE IN THE WORLD IS NORDEAST?

Perhaps Northeast Minneapolis can best be pictured as a quarter of a pie. The tip of it points to the East Hennepin and Main Street intersection. One side would be stretching north along the Mississippi, while the other side would stretch along Hennepin Avenue eastward. From those two edges the interior begins to fill up, spreading north and east from former farm fields and woods to present areas of industry, homes, and schools.

Settled initially by the French, the town of St. Anthony spread along the river before it was annexed into Minneapolis in 1872. Its ever-widening dirt roads, (which became our main drags) expanded in and out of old areas. Immigrants settled here and sent letters back home to European countries, encouraging others to come over for the many common labor jobs needing filling. Wars spread the word as well. The myriad ethnic churches springing up everywhere— and we do mean everywhere —provided relatives and others shelter from storms they might be facing in their countries.

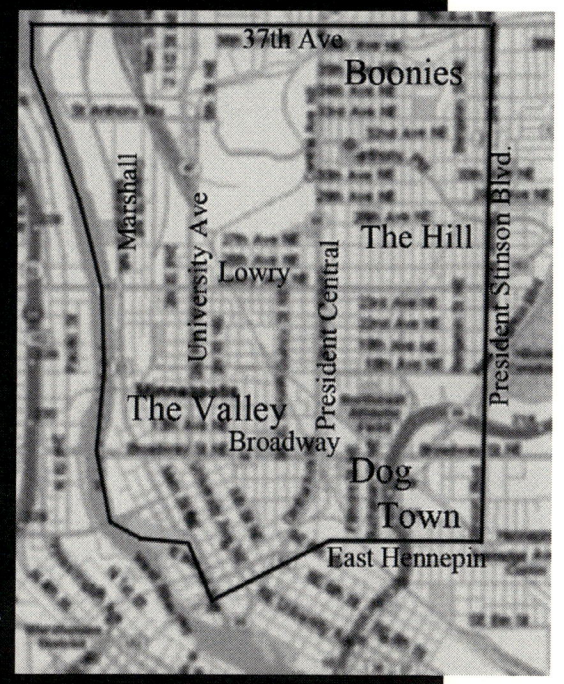

With more people and housing, streets became established to fill in amongst the main dirt roads of Main, Central, Broadway (45th parallel, N. Latitude), and University.

(Continued on page 4)

CLASS BACKWARDS — CHAPTER ONE

(Continued from page 3)
The new streets and avenues, some of them named after United States Presidents, provided a number system and a structure. Throw in Stinson and St. Anthony Boulevards, Brighton Avenue and Brighton Boulevard, as well as the many parks laid out by Theodore Wirth, and we had a means of finding our way around.

Looking across river at Minneapolis from the St. Anthony side

Nordeast kids learned United States history at a tender age. Immigrants found that naming streets after presidents worked to their advantage as well. The early heavily traveled dirt roads hung onto their names. Other slight modifications of names were made. Fittingly, Harrison named for William Henry Harrison – who only lived a month in office – became the shortest street turning into Central. Names were not duplicated. John Quincy Adams became Quincy. Due to duplication elsewhere, Grant became Ulysses. Benjamin Harrison became Benjamin. Highway 8 and cemeteries held back the grid and they ran out of streets just as they ran out of Presidents. Coolidge was the last. **Bob Buntrock**

Of course we didn't know of this background, nor did it really matter, since it was already there as we were growing up. For some of us, it was confusing.

CHAPTER - ONE   CLASS BACKWARDS

I didn't grow up "Nordeast." Although we had moved to the north and east of the Mississippi river by the time of my earliest memories, I was the son of an English teacher who would tolerate nothing but the clearest of pronunciations. So we lived in North-East. I didn't even know about Nordeast until I reached my junior high school years at Edison. **Larry Kohout**

There is the fact that one learns the order to the Presidents from living there. That's one thing that has helped me to always remember their order. However, I never found any information on President Central or President Stinson Boulevard. Did anyone else? **Bev Warren**

We lived within a half-block of the eastern city limits and within five blocks of the northern city limits. My parents' friends felt they needed to pack a lunch if they were to visit us in the boonies. **Larry Kohout**

CLASS BACKWARDS — CHAPTER ONE

The streets of Northeast Minneapolis are referred to as a good way to learn the Presidents. However, growing up in lower Northeast and living on 2nd Street and then Broadway & 4th Street, I did not really have any reason to go beyond Monroe. So any order or even acknowledgement that the rest of the presidents were further up did not really occur to me. I remember once, in 8th grade, visiting my Aunt and Uncle on Benjamin. I walked to the Hollywood Theatre for a movie, and got lost. When heading home I passed or missed Benjamin and seeing Arthur and Cleveland I decided the streets were alphabetical. That only made it worse because Benjamin did not appear. Finally, I asked someone and got headed in the right direction. Upon arriving back at my Aunt and Uncle's home, their only comment to my dilemma was "Don't you know your Presidents?" I did begin to learn them when I finally attended Edison. So more presidents stuck in my head, not necessarily in order. And I knew they were not alphabetical. But I soon found that many of the kids lived on what they called the "Hill." Now I had to remember that I lived in "The Valley"—which I never knew! In spite of this lack of knowledge, I did graduate. **Rod Nelson**

Hollywood Theater—circa 1950

Nordeast is Beautiful

Back in 1972, there was an article in the Sunday Minneapolis Tribune about Northeast Minneapolis. According to Robert T. Smith, a columnist for the Minneapolis Tribune, "Some folks in that area didn't like it. The article depicted Northeast as a place where people are said to be hard-working, hard-drinking, a little less well educated than average, and conservative in their beliefs."

Smith explained, "Well, it wasn't the hard-working tag they objected to."

Three well-known fellows from the area, Jack Kozlak and Harold Kalina, both state legislators from Northeast and Northeast-raised University of Minnesota vice-president Stanley Wenberg offered to take Smith for a ride and show him what Northeast Minneapolis was really like.

After the tour, Smith wanted to make it clear that he wasn't saying those fellows were exaggerating, but after spending all afternoon with them, he was forced to conclude that:

- There has never been a fight in Northeast Minneapolis.
- Alcohol is only taken internally to cure leprosy.
- All Northeast residents were either bankers, lawyers, or university vice-presidents.

There was one glitch when they took him to Danny's Bar. Smith noted that "All was peaceful. The patrons were listening to a symphony emanating from a color TV set in a corner."

He went on, "As the barman approached, I asked: 'How many fights have you had in here lately?'

He appeared astounded. 'None,' he said. 'We never have fights in here.'

(Continued on page 8)

(Continued from page 7)

'You mean there's never been a fight here?' I countered.

'No,' he said. 'We have them outside.' "

Smith concluded what he really wanted to say about Northeast:

"It is a neighborhood of Old World charm, a place unique in Minneapolis and a location that should be cherished for its flavor. My argument about its faults, for me, is irrelevant. The idea that Northeast types cling to their European heritage is very appealing. The knowledge that Northeast is a town in itself, that it has much of the advantages of a small community including the fact that everybody seems to know everybody, is something to exploit.

"They still perform Old World native dances; they still, in many cases, bake their own bread; they still observe the Russian New Year on 4th Street N.E., and other traditional festivals. And, they still have a feeling for their area that does not exist much anymore in this modern age, they are intensely proud of Northeast, and that pride does not leave them even when they leave."

He added that his tour guides explained that people who live or once lived in Northeast, preserved their European heritage. It has been a town that everybody comes home to, a hard-working community where people look after each other. The fierce pride of the Northeast residents no doubt makes them a bit adverse to criticism. One of the things they didn't like was the label "Nordeast."

Smith concluded, "Sometimes it gets hilarious. In rebuttal to the Tribune report concerning the questionable use of Nordeast, buttons and bumper stickers are selling well in Northeast. And what do they say?

'Nordeast is Beautiful.'

You have to kind of admire that."

CHAPTER TWO:
LESSONS FROM THE PAST

We were born in America, children of the early '40s. Our parents and relatives went through The Depression of the '30s. We heard stories of how our families and people that we knew had gone through hard times before us and learned from them.

They knew poverty, so we were taught that wearing hand-me-down clothes while we were children was never an embarrassment, but something we did with pride. We made-do with what we had. Waste was considered a sin. We were told to clean our plate because there were starving children all over the world. A basic characteristic of living as we did was a humbleness of spirit, almost a reverse form of snobbery. We were skeptical of anything too rich or too showy. We looked after each other and helped those in need.

Left to right David and Glen Larson, and Joey Tapsak

Depression

Long after the Depression — Our homes still had signs that something had happened. It lasted into our early years of growing up. Some of us did some bagging up of grain or coal that fell off train cars to bring home to feed the chickens or to add to the coal pile. The coal was pretty rough and we were told we shouldn't burn it. It was called slag or something like that. Soap bar scraps were tossed into a large jar to make more soap later. **Rod Nelson**

CLASS BACKWARDS — CHAPTER · TWO

Storing Food — I remember my dad never lost his fear of being poor. Some of this came from his upbringing, but many of these fears came from going through the Depression. In our home, we had a root cellar in our basement. We would stack the shelves with canned goods, and whenever we were low on food, my dad would worry and go to the store to fill them up again. **Carol Lyons Larson**

Lard Sandwiches — I can remember my Mom, (born in 1920) saying she and her brother had to eat lard and sugar sandwiches for lunch during the Depression. **Judy Sheldon Johnson**

Doing Without — The things that come to mind after the Depression: We relied on home canning, like fruits, tomatoes, pickles. We didn't have many cakes or cookies because sugar was in short supply. Buying/wearing shoes that didn't fit, because they were cheaper. We mended clothes, not buying new, and wore hand-me-downs, wherever we could get them. No vacations.

We stretched the food budget. On Tuesdays, we ate waffles with ½ slice of bacon on top for supper. We had ration stamps: little pink ones. **Carolyn Jodie Hagford**

CHAPTER - TWO   CLASS BACKWARDS

Helping Each Other— There was a little "Mom and Pop" store on 5th street between 15th & 17th Avenues. The couple was Jewish and my parents used to go there for odds and ends, like milk & bread. The couple was very understanding of the times and often allowed our family and many others to charge their goods and pay them when the customers also received their paychecks. They turned out to be best friends to my parents.

We raised chickens in our back yard and Mother sold eggs to anyone in the neighborhood who wanted them but not least, being the only girl in the family, I got to wear all my brothers 'hand me downs'. I was always thrilled when Christmas came around because I always got a new dress and a new pair of p.j.'s. Can't beat those flannel PJs.
Jan Miskowiec Anweiller

Necessary Skills — Making do was darning holes in socks, making rags from old items, crocheting doilies, sewing or mending clothes. This work kept my mother busy until we were taught how to help out with some of it. A sewing machine was ready to go and a basket of mending was always there. Mother had learned these skills growing up and doing them for her mother and siblings. I did enjoy learning how to do many of these things from her. I could use those skills today. **Rod Nelson**

Rationing — My parents were farmers and I was born in Le Sueur, MN. Moved to Big Lake, MN in 1943. Moved to 1306 Central Avenue N.E. in 1944. There was rationing of many things. **Ray Miller**

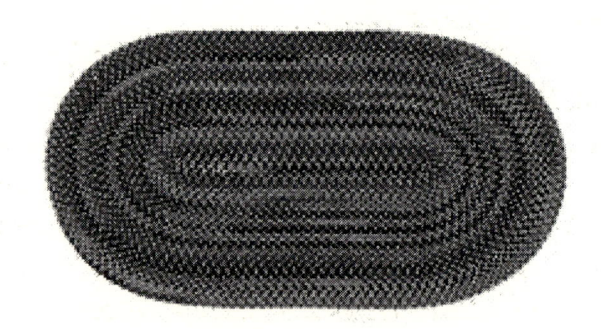

Losses — During the Depression, my parents never bought a house of their own because they were afraid prices would collapse in another Depression. My mother made rugs from old nylons braided and sewn together. We ate terrible margarine with little yellow capsules of dye in the packages that we'd crush. Next we'd knead the bag until it was pretty much uniformly yellow. My father lost his gas station in Fort Dodge, Iowa, due to rationing, and he moved us up to Minneapolis when I was 2 because there were jobs at the Northern Pump, the munitions plant. **Louie Paff**

How We Handled the Depression

Money Was Scarce — My father came to the U.S. from Norway in 1927, just two years before the Depression. He had $25 in his pocket and didn't speak English. He worked at various jobs (once told the employment office that he could do carpentry, then when he got the job, the guy he was working for said, "You don't know anything about carpentry, do you?") Somehow he survived in New York City and got free college at the City College of New York. He came to Minnesota to go to

(Continued on page 13)

(Continued from page 12)

dental school after he had saved enough money for tuition. He was always very careful with money. He and my mother met at the start of dental school, but didn't get married until he had finished. She was a nurse, and used her savings to buy him dental equipment. When they finally bought a house years later (the one I grew up in on St. Anthony Blvd.), they borrowed pretty much the whole amount ($12,000) but had it paid off within 10 years. During the rest of their lives, they saved up for anything they bought, and usually paid for everything with cash, even after credit cards became popular after World War II.

Norm Solberg

Sharing Groceries —
Gas rationing was a part of WWII and pretty much kept a lot of people off the road. We were lucky as kids because every Sunday we got to spend hours on the road because of our Dad's access to gas. He owned trucks which delivered canned food, cereal, soaps, and everything else to grocery stores. We just cruised around the Twin Cities on Sunday afternoon so Dad could let his drivers know what time to start Monday morning. Of course, this included a stop at the A&W on Central Avenue between Lowry and 26th Avenue. The Coneys were pretty good back then. I think the secret was in the Lard they used to cook the hamburger for the sauce.

Every few months our Dad would bring home a truck and back it into our backyard on a Sunday night. It had a load of damaged

(Continued on page 14)

(Continued from page 13)

canned goods and other supplies from the warehouse. Dad would go down in the basement and our Grandfather or one of our uncles would bring the cases to one of the basement windows and put it through to my Dad who would but it on pallets. We asked Dad why they were doing that and he said it was because they, "had to get the stuff before the hoarders got it," then he would laugh. Actually, the foods were not just for us, but were given to a lot of our relatives and for people our parents knew who were down on their luck Our Dad was an excellent student at Edison but in the 11th grade (1929), our grandfather decided it was best for him to go to work. So at 16, Dad was driving truck for the company our Grandfather worked as the warehouse superintendent. Two years later, our uncle had to do the same. It could have been thought of as a bad break but both our dad and uncle ended up helping start wholesale grocery companies both becoming warehouse superintendents and each owning a fleet of trucks. So the Depression was bad for some and it turned out to be lucky for them (us). Our mother graduated from Edison in 1933 and was never able to find a job anywhere. She ended up taking care of some children and keeping house for a family in the neighborhood. Then she married our dad and got a lifetime job raising us. I think she would have liked doing anything else. I know just about anything else would be a lot easier.   **Gordie Solz**

World Wars I and II

Almost every family had someone who defended our country in World Wars I and II. We were proud of our flag and what it symbolized. Patriotic songs were on the radio and donations were gathered in the movie theaters for the war effort. Radio and movie news provided stories of bombings and fighting that was far away from where we lived. As small tots we were too young to have understood what these events really meant, but indications that our relatives were fighting in the wars made us cling closely to our family and our home.

CHAPTER TWO   **CLASS BACKWARDS**

World War I — Soon after World War I broke out, my father enlisted in the Army to obtain his U.S. citizenship. He was sent to France and fought in the Battle of Chateau-Thierry in 1918. We still have his uniformed photo from WWI, gas-mask and all. After he was wounded in France, and honorably discharged, he returned and ended up in Minneapolis. Gratefully, he received wonderful care at the Veteran's Hospital. **Athena Dascalos**

Athena's father

Service Banners — We had a little silk-fringed banner hung in a window of our house. When I asked what it was for mother said that it meant someone from the family was in the service. When I walked down the streets, I then began to notice them in other windows as well. **Rod Nelson**

Everyone Had a Part — My brothers and I would take cans of grease to the local butcher on 15th and Washington St., N.E. Why did we have to do that? As of now I don't remember but it was a requirement the US government put out during the "war years." The cans would be like when you opened a can of veggies, rinse out the can and pour the grease into it. Otherwise we would crush the cans for the war effort.

Men who had families were the last to be called up. I can remember my dad going

(Continued on page 16)

(Continued from page 15)

down to get his physical. Fortunately, for us, my dad didn't pass the test because he had a heart condition that prevented him from going into the service.

If you had someone in your family who was in the military, you put a star in your window. I had several aunts and uncles who were in the military. I remember "troop trains" coming by the house as we lived next to an empty field and the train tracks were on the other side of the field. The troops would throw boxes of cookies to us while we stood there and waved to them.   **Janet Miskowiec Anweiller**

Rod Nelson with his aunt

Penny & Polly Grivna with their aunt

Posters and Slogans Were Everywhere — My Dad was never drafted (although he came close) so my memories of WW II are that of a small child with my family at home. I had several cousins, most male and all older. The guys were all in service and we kept track of their exploits. One cousin was with Clark's Armored Division in France and Germany including the Battle of the Bulge. Two other cousins were in the Seabees in the South Pacific. Another cousin was (and is to this day) a pilot. He flew P-51s and was about to be deployed for the invasion of Japan when the war ended. Another cousin, with both brothers in service, was turned down in '44 for poor eyesight, started college, but was drafted right after VE Day into the OSS. He helped with intelligence in post-war Europe with his proficiency in German. After a BA and MS in Political Science, he joined the State Department (probably the CIA, really).

Dad was a block captain in Civil Defense and I vaguely remember bombing drills, including an exercise at

(Continued on page 17)

(Continued from page 16)

Pillsbury School with a simulation of it being bombed. These drills were quite frightening to a 3-4 year old. I also remember blackout shades and rationing.

I don't remember food rationing but we had gardens (Victory Gardens, I guess) both in the back yard and in the vacant lot across the street where we grew much of our food. Later I read Dad's civil defense material and discovered more of the fears of being bombed although Hitler never did have anything capable of bombing us.

Posters, slogans like "Buy War Bonds" were everywhere. We even saw reminders at church. Lutheran World Relief was quite active worldwide especially in the South Pacific. There was a picture of a small LWR hospital ship in our church basement. When I asked my dad what it was, he said it had been torpedoed by the Japanese during their invasion of Indonesia, even though it was well identified as a hospital ship.

I don't remember V-E Day but I do remember the Hiroshima bomb. We were visiting my aunt and uncle east of Sandstone and while waiting in the train station to return home, my Dad and someone were talking about something quite serious. When I asked Dad what they were talking about, he said something about a mysterious powerful bomb and he didn't know much more. As I got older, the impact of the war was more memorable. **Bob Buntrock**

Music and Memories — Mother had a small table-top radio that she had on much of the day. I still can identify with that time when today I hear war songs of that period. Songs like: *Rainbow at Midnight, Coming in on a Wing and a Prayer, K-k-k-katie, Mademoiselle from Armetiers, Boogie Woogie Bugle Boy*. Not 'till later did I learn that many of the songs were revived from WWI. But hearing the words made me aware that War (however important that was) was happening someplace and Dad, Uncle, or Aunt had to go. **Rod Nelson**

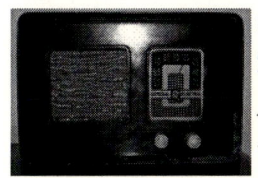

Songs On the Radio — I don't remember any of the songs etc. to remind me of the war. I would at times listen to the radio about the action going on with the war. There was rationing of many things. That's about it. **Ray Miller**

Rod Nelson's uncle

Families Lived Together — Perhaps I have a poor long-term memory, but I really don't remember the War. My mother and I followed Daddy to Newfoundland at the beginning, but then when Pearl Harbor was bombed, all dependents were sent back home. My mom told me that she was very anxious on the ship, wondering if we would be safe. Mom and I then went to live with her parents on the farm in Sauk Rapids. It was a true extended family affair. My grandparents, my mom, me and my aunt, whose husband was also in the war, and another aunt and uncle were all living in that house.

I had a pet lamb and loved to play with the dog and 'visit' with the cows and horses. To this day I am a huge animal lover. I saw my dad only once during those four years. I think it was hard for him to come back and get to know a little girl who had grown so much. After that, we bought our home on 22nd Avenue and stayed there until that very sad day when Daddy was transferred to Pennsylvania after my graduation. We all did not want to leave Minnesota. **Mary Ann Tema Weinberger**

CHAPTER - TWO — CLASS BACKWARDS

SAVING TINFOIL — Another memory I have of World War II was saving tin foil. Little bits of tinfoil from chewing gum, cigarette packages, some candy wrappers, and food wrappers were rolled up, little by little, into a big ball. All the neighbors would turn in their tinfoil ball to the local settlement house on Saturday nights. All of the balls were then given to a representative from one of the services. We were told that these tinfoil balls would all be gathered together and melted down to help with metal parts for weapons. **Bob Peters**

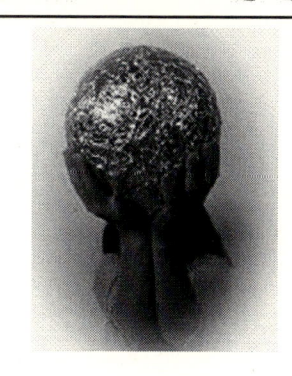

Popeye — One time when my dad and his brother both came home for a leave, they dressed Grandpa up in a white navy uniform for photos. He was very proud of his sons. But he looked like "Popeye the Sailor Man" and everyone burst out laughing. **Rod Nelson**

Rod Nelson's Grandfather

White Gas — I was pretty young, but I can remember my dad going into the Army in 1943. He went to Maryland for training and then off to the Pacific Theater. He was in a combat engineering outfit and went from New Guinea through the Philippines and onto Japan after the bombs were dropped. We had a 1941 Chevrolet when dad left and gas was rationed so my mother found that white gas was available and drove the car on that until the engine went bad. White gas burned very hot and caused the engine to fail. Dad returned in February 1946 and things took a while but got back to normal. He bought a 1940 used Hudson and in June of 1949, we drove to Oakland California with only two breakdowns. We were living in Columbia Heights at the time and moved to Polk Street in June of 1950. **Dick Sherwood.**

'41 Chevy coup

Extended Families — Our grandmother and grandfather (on our mother's side) owned their house on Spring and Monroe Street for over 50 years. During the war years, as many as 35 people (all relatives) lived in that three bedroom house. Our mother had 10 brothers and sisters and the youngest four still lived at home along with the wives of some of the older brothers with their children because our uncles were all overseas in the Navy or Army. Almost every one of the adults were working either days or nights which allowed everyone to have a place to sleep when they came home because of the different shifts. Grandma made lunch for around 20 everyday because most of the kids brought their friends over to play and if they were there, they got lunch too. I remember the yard didn't have a blade of grass because they were constantly running around and playing games.
Gordie Solz

The Significance of War

Worthwhile Sacrifices — Growing up I don't think many of us knew the significance of what was happening, how different the world would have been - in the worst imaginable way – if it were not for the sacrifice made by that greatest generation. My dad had two brothers who served in the military during the war: one in the Marine Corps in the Pacific and one in the Navy. I knew this because my grandmother had a small cloth banner in the window with two stars on it. There were rationing books with stamps for sugar, butter and other stuff I don't remember.

Many of us had wooden military-like rifles, and playing war was a game. We even dug foxholes in a nearby empty lot. There were the Movietone News and war movies. I vaguely remember a practice blackout. I knew the war was over when my uncle spent his first night back from military service at our house. I remember him appearing late at night in his Marine uniform.

Ironically, my biggest sacrifice to the war came in 1958, when I had a 1950 Chevy with synthetic rubber inner tubes (real rubber was not available during the war). I had at least six flat tires (one in the Sun Drive-In) before I scraped up enough money to replace them. **Dick Myslajek**

CHAPTER · TWO CLASS BACKWARDS

Black Outs — One thing I remember about the war was my dad's yellow helmet. He was the neighborhood captain. I don't know what all of his responsibilities were but I do remember he was responsible for organizing a practice blackout – all lights out or windows covered. Fortunately, we never needed to have a real blackout.   **Jim Terry (class of 1956)**

The End of The War

Finally Over — I was listening to our Philco radio standing in the corner of our living room. All of sudden the program was interrupted, and I could hear nothing but static and strange garbled voices. My Mom rushed in and called my sister into the living room. The three of us stood looking at the radio. I looked up and saw my mom and sister both crying, so I figured it was bad news. But instead, some music started playing, and they both hugged each other, jumping up and down in joy. 'The War is over!' they chanted. 'The War is over!' They were whooping with happiness and so I did too, not understanding a word of what it meant. For me, at 5 years old, in my house, and in my neighborhood, World War II with its volatile ending was very far away, but I was happy because they were happy. **Carol Lyons Larson**

Cooking Over An Open Fire — After the War, there would be hobos camped along the tracks. We would venture up to 37th Avenue and walk along the railroad tracks. I can still recall the man in the bushy white beard who was cooking something over an open fire. He seemed old at the time but I'm not so sure of that anymore. It seemed like quite an adventure to be riding the rails traveling the country although we were oblivious to the hardships these poor people faced. **Dodd Knutson (Class of '59)**

A Big Celebration — I was five years old when the war in Europe ended. Nevertheless, I have some very strong memories of the end of the war. Our family was living on Arthur Street between 32nd and 33rd Avenues, and our next-door neighbors were the Johnsons whose son, Jim, turned out to be a classmate.

You may remember that the end of the Second World War in Europe occurred on May 8, 1945. It just so happens that my birthday also falls on May 8th. Mother had arranged a party for me with a number of my friends in attendance. We were all outside playing when all of a sudden we began hearing the whistles of trains in the Soo Line yard. It was not unusual to hear the whistle designating end of shift from the Soo Line but it was very unusual to hear that whistle along with several train whistles all going off simultaneously and with such a sustained blast. Shortly after this noise began people began throwing open their doors and yelling. Passing cars began honking their horns for extended periods and general pandemonium existed throughout the neighborhoods.

My mother tried to explain that the war in Europe had ended. My friends may have believed this but I knew better. Everyone was helping celebrate my birthday. **Larry Kohout**

CHAPTER THREE:
OUR HERITAGE - GRANDMA WORE A BABUSHKA

Many of our relatives came from the Old Country meaning in this case, Eastern or Western Europe. Relatives often lived on the same block. It was a potluck dinner, as though we were bringing our heritage to the table. Each ethnic group that came to live here brought their own kind of flavor to the final menu: French, German, Italian, Polish, Russian, Irish, Lebanese, Greek, Native Americans, Scandinavian and more. There were so many ethnic groups, some affectionately referred to our area as Little Europe. Many just called it Nordeast Minneapolis. We were the children and grandchildren of the immigrants who came for a better life. We had a distinct identity from the rest of the city. An area that was easy for immigrants to be welcomed and to settle in. We were what we were. Nothing fancy. Just a buffet of interesting people.

Boxcar Child — I barely knew my grandfather. It was said that he was a boxcar child when he came to Minneapolis and was adopted. He was of Irish and Scandinavian descent and married a French woman who died before I was born. Dad always had a great deal of love and loyalty to both sides of his growing up family. **Rod Nelson**

Babushka — Both of my grandmothers wore babushkas, and on occasion my mother would wear one also – especially if she was outside in the cold. It seems like a good way to keep your head warm. I think they will eventually come back into fashion. **Dick Myslajek**

Ellis Island Naming — My maternal grandmother was Norwegian, but my grandfather was an orphan and was Dutch. When he arrived in Ellis Island, they gave him the "Vandermyde" name, which meant his family came from a meadow or a market. **John Vandermyde**

Czechoslovakia — My parents were both from a small village in Czechoslovakia, and immigrated to Minneapolis, around 1919. Due to the Immigration Laws at the time, my parents came to the U.S.A. separately. My father around 1919, and my mother, brother, and sister came seven years later, after my father established the requirements needed to allow his family to join him. I'm not sure of the date that my parents became United States citizens, but I do know that Dave Larson's mom tutored my mom in English and helped her pass the test. I was born at home, on Sept. 19th 1939, at 2651 7th Street, N.E. Minneapolis.
Joe Kohanik

My Bohemian, Scottish, English, German, Background — Dad always said he was a "dukes mixture" and no one could figure out what that was. He was wrong. His paternal grandfather and grandmother were both full blooded Bohemians (the Czech Republic today). The name Kohout is Bohemian for "rooster." Freely translated it is the equivalent of the English name "Farmer." On his maternal side, his grandfather was (as fully as I've been able to trace it) a Scot. That side of the family always claimed to be related to Robert Burns, the poet. One of my uncles is even named Robert Burns Kohout. However, I had to let them know that the family of their heritage was in the US before the poet was born. Dad's maternal grandmother was born in England.

As kids we always were told we were 3/4 German and the other quarter, "God Only Knows." As it turned out the only German we have is through my mother whose father was a full blooded German, making us 25% German.

Mom's mother always said she was full blooded German. When I traced it out she was a full blooded Dutch. I've traced her family back to 1655 and that family was always in Limbricht, Limburg, Netherlands up until my great grandfather immigrated to the US in 1862. The really funny thing is that she always made rather disparaging comments about the Dutch. **Larry Kohout**

Germany - Researching My Genealogy —
Grandparents on my mother's side came from Germany as young people. My grandfather came from Hessen, and my grandmother came from Ausfriesland, only about 20 miles from the North Sea. As an aside I know and get together with about 30 relatives in Germany on my grandfather's side. On my father's side you have to go back to my great-grandparents. My great-grandfather Pfaff *also* came from Hessen to Wisconsin. He lived only about 40 miles from where my mother's father came from! My great-grandmother Goetz came from Hessen, about 10 miles from where my great-grandfather was born, but they didn't meet until they were in Wisconsin. In that sense it was a small world for them. I know and get together with seven relatives in Germany from my great-grandfather's side.

Why did they all come here from Germany? In a phrase: poverty in Germany in the 1800s. Because each family divided their farmland among their offspring, and with each succeeding generation the farms became smaller until it got to a point there wasn't enough land to make a living. So in the 1800s there were huge numbers of unemployed people in Germany, and making the move to America became a very attractive idea. I have letters from my maternal grandfather's side in Germany in the 1800s describing the poverty and also the diseases. There are phrases such as, "the children are getting over their diphtheria now," "a cousin died from cholera," "Maria died a horrible death from a disease in which she couldn't move her jaw," (sounds like tetanus to me), and a thank you to my grandfather for sending his brother, wife, and two children $10, which allowed them to eat meat for the first time in five months. **Louie Paff**

Sweden —
My grandmother, my mother's mother, came from Sweden. She was born in 1880. At age 12 she had to take a boat by herself and arrived at Ellis Island in 1893, with her name and destination around her neck. She finally came to Northeast Minneapolis to stay with her grandparents, working for Wheeler Wilson, a sewing machine company. She stayed there until she married my grandfather. So my mother was full-blooded Swedish. My dad's family came from Norway. **Anita Wiggen Monette**

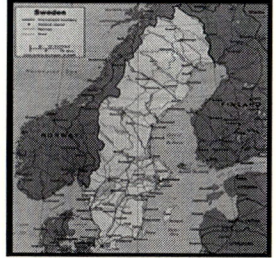

Greece — My mother's parents, James and Mary Manthis, emigrated from Chryssafa, Greece, a village outside of Sparta, in the Peloponnese in 1897. The family lived in Chicago, where my grandfather had a grocery store and raised 7 out of 9 children. Later they moved to Minneapolis where my mother Kalliope (Edna) was born in 1916 and her sister Aphrodite followed shortly after. My father, James M. Dascalos, was born in 1898 in a tobacco-growing village in Dimena, Greece (south of Corinth). He and his brother, John, emigrated to the U.S.A. in 1916. They bought their first house at 3159 Johnson Street, N.E. and raised four daughters, who attended Thomas Lowry and Edison. While in High School, the family moved to 2301 Roosevelt Street N.E. until it was sold in 2009. **Athena Dascalos**

What's In A Name — Whether by accident or on purpose or by necessity, many of the family names of immigrants were changed in the new country. Some because of differences in alphabets or the sounds of letters; some purely by accident upon entering the country at Ellis Island; and some did it on purpose to shorten a long name with lots of unpronounceable letters, or to "Americanize their name." For instance, Sharon Matt's original name was Matwejeic and Anita Wiggen's name was Vigen. **Dick Myslajek**

Grandparents — My grandparents had the same name. **Ray Miller**

Lebanon Roots of Royalty — Both of my sets of grandparents had emigrated eventually to N.E. Minneapolis from Lebanon. My mother's side (Saba) left Beirut and stayed in South America for the first two years. My father's parents were from a farming village. His dad had passed away and Grandmother remarried Aneen Simon. (Actually the name Simon was given in the process of immigrating from the Name Soluum.) At that time, war was the reason for leaving. My great grandmother on my mother's side

(Continued on page 27)

(Continued from page 26)

had already moved to N.E.

St. Maron's Church was the supporting service for our community.

I can remember Grandfather Jacob who had red hair and had been a professor in Beirut sitting in the back yard with the other neighborhood men. They would all be patiently waiting their turn while Grandfather translated the English to Arabic and vice versa for them. Grandmother Jacob was always in the kitchen cooking up something, especially flatbread. I can still recall the fresh bread we talked her into giving us direct from the heavily floured table and hot stove. Her nine children kept her busy. My Dad's mother raised her five kids alone after her second husband Aneen passed away. Besides all parenting chores, she also did some "domestic" type of work in the neighborhood to bring in a little money. Her oldest son worked as well to help support my dad's family growing up.

Dad and mom most likely met at St. Maron's Church. They had a lot of activities for our community. They could have met at the Simon's store that eventually opened in the neighborhood. Our upbringing was very strict, but fair. A strong look from Dad or a "Wait 'til your father gets home," from Mom was all it really took. Our religion was a very important part of our daily life as well.

One final thought is about a Star Tribune news article that appeared when I was young regarding our ancestry back in Lebanon. Further back, as cousins married cousins, to keep the properties in the families, our lineage shows that we came from Royalty. Well, once my friends found out about that I was heavily teased about it. It may be true, but none of our family has been asked to come back to Lebanon to rule. **Ginny Simon Erickson**

Making It In a New Country

The Solz Family Name — Our Great-Grandfather Amelio Santangelo and Great-Grandmother Palenccia Santangelo came to the United States on April 15, 1898 bringing our Grandfather Emidio (6 years old) and his sister Marianina Domencia (12 years old) from Pietrabbondante, Italy. His half brother Valentino DiSalvo (21 years old) came with them and they all came on the Kaiser Wilhelm II to Ellis Island in New

(Continued on page 28)

Italy
(Continued from page 27)

York and then went to live in Duluth, Minnesota. At that time Italians were not at all well thought of in the U.S. Our family has thought the reason the name was changed was two-fold: that Italians were second or third class citizens and also that they wanted to be Americans. Ameilio Santangelo took the name Emil Solz, his wife was called Palma, Emidio became Ed Solz and Marianina was called Mamie Solz. Our Great-Great Uncle Valentino DiSalvo took the name Walter Dodge. Emil and Walter all became successful buying and selling property in Duluth leaving behind substantial estates. Just a note- When Emil Solz died in 1941 he left his son Ed and daughters Mamie and Pauly (born after their arrival in Duluth) $10 each and to his grandson Clarence he left apartment buildings, duplexes and four-plexes with a large amount of cash. The reason was Clarence (DiSalvo) Dodge married Rose Mancini who his Grandfather Emil had lined up for him by his brother Tony Santangelo in Wooster, Ohio. Great-Grandfather Emil also had ladies to marry our father Art Solz, our Uncles Mike Solz and Don Solz. They all declined. **Gordie Solz**

The Arone Family — Here is what I remember I was told: My father's parents came here from Padua, Italy in the 1890's. Names were changed because there was so much prejudice. "WOP" originally meant "Without Passport." Michael worked for the city of Minneapolis and passed away in 1914 during a bad flu epidemic. Virginia was a seamstress and lived with our family until she died in 1968.

My father, James, was on the Highway Patrol when that organization first started in 1929 and later became a detective with the Minneapolis Police Department, until 1946 when he bought the Pine Tavern in NE Minneapolis. His brother Ralph was a Minneapolis Fireman until retirement. Two other children died in infancy. My mother, Edith, was born on a farm in Upsala, Minnesota and James and Edith were married in 1934. **Mike Arone**

Poland

Bilingual — My mother was born in Poland. She came to the U.S. at nine months old. Her schooling was an eighth grade education. She spoke fluent English and Polish. I regret that I never learned to speak Polish. She was a homemaker and didn't drive. **Nancy Olson Tanner**

Polack — Contrary to common belief, "Polack" is not a derogatory term (although it may have been in some circles.) In the Polish language, Polak (male, nominative case) identifies a male of Polish descent. I never heard the term Polack except by my father who gave it to me as a nickname. It was never meant to be taken in anything but a positive way. **Dick Myslajek**

> **My uncle was Polish** — My uncle was Polish so maybe there was a general acceptance of the use of "Polack" in a non-derogatory or a kidding way if you were Polish. I heard it a lot. I didn't know one group from another and at early single digit years of age probably didn't even know what a 'Polack' was as well. Do wonder now how welcomed the use was just as with other ethnic group names of the times. Certainly there were times when ethnic referrals were cause for a good fight. **Rod Nelson**

Time Well Spent — My great-grandmother (Prussian/Polish/German) did visit us from Melrose where that side of the family immigrated. She took a great deal of pride in our being raised as Catholics and was here for those special days. When we visited her in Melrose, she was always busy washing clothes, gardening, or cooking. Her house was very dark during the day maybe to save electricity. She spoke very little English. But mother was still able to speak some German with her. Mother had spent many summers as a young girl with her Grandmother.
Rod Nelson

Lessons Learned From My Grandparents — My growing up was colored by my grandparents' views of the world. I learned about frugality, cooking, and honest work, to name a few. My grandfather was born in Poland of Lithuanian parents; my grandmother was Polish but born in Germany. They were 21 years apart in age. It was an arranged marriage, and those differences created interesting situations that held life-long lessons for me.

My father's father built duplexes and rented them – even to our family. His home was one room on the first floor of the duplex we lived in, but upstairs. When his work took him to St. Paul, he would walk there and back home to Northeast Minneapolis—each day— carrying his tools. I found out the reason – he didn't want to spend the five cents for the streetcar fare. When he died, we found a brown leather coin purse in his drawer, packed with pennies. Was this his idea of frugality? I saw—and learned.

Bob Peters' Grandparents

Because of his Old World ways, as soon as Grandfather realized that I was left-handed, he tried to change this. Every time he saw me with a pencil or piece of chalk in my 'wrong' hand, he would gently slap that hand while saying bad, bad. I saw, I felt – and I never wanted him to see me write.

Often I would travel down the alley to visit my grandmother. She usually was cooking. She also worked in downtown Minneapolis cleaning offices at night to help raise her five children. Long and tiring work for her, but it was honest work. My grandma also took me places, downtown to eat at Nankin, the Chinese Restaurant, to Witt's grocery store on Hennepin Avenue, and even on a train trip all the way to California for my aunt's wedding. Grandpa showed me how to plant a garden and he and I took long walks together, looking at the land. I learned from my grandparents, whether good or bad, by watching what they did and how they lived.
Bob Peters

A Menu of Memories

Slovakia — My grandparents came from Slovakia. My grandmother spoke to us in her native tongue, but that was different from the language spoken in church. Thus, I could understand nothing of what was said. But, I remember sitting in one of the front pews every Sunday with my Grandparents, seemingly enjoying being there. I guess because it was the thing to do.
Penny Grivna Peters

> **Tradition** — Traditional food, religion, language, music, weddings and holidays are what I remember most about my heritage – perhaps as much or more from my grandparents as my parents. All of my grandparents immigrated from Poland and I was lucky enough to share time with all of them. They were all bilingual but reverted to Polish when conversing with each other. Polish was taught in parochial schools in their time (Holy Cross and St. Hedwig's). Because of this I can get the drift of a conversation in Polish and understand common words (golobkie, kapusta, kielbasa, pierogi, pevo, etc).
>
> **Music** — Music was important. My paternal grandfather played the tuba at neighborhood band concerts, having played in a Polish army band before immigrating. The first music I remember were polkas and marches my father played on a small 78 rpm phonograph.
>
> **Anna** — Anna, my maternal grandmother. came to America for a better life and lived through two wars and the Great Depression. So the lesson was be frugal and waste nothing. Without much formal education – she learned sewing at a convent in Poland. Yet with nothing more than my grandfather's labor wages, she bought, rented and sold properties and ultimately financed my father into a small business. She was an expert at practical things: making bread, sewing, gardening and getting by. She was the best of cooks but my fondest memories were of the homemade soups and homemade bread. I would get the first slice, the warm scrika (heal) with butter and honey. I do miss that! **Dick Myslajek**

From Russia To A New Life In Northeast — My early years did not begin like all the other girls in Northeast. I was born in Russia in a small resort town known as Belarenchenskia on the Black Sea on October 13, 1940. The climate was quite warm and we had Palm Trees, actually, the climate was very much like where I live now in Mesa, Az. My father was Russian and my mother was Ukrainian. They were educated people. My father was a Locomotive Engineer (a very prestigious occupation in Russia) and my mother was a Pharmacist.

My dad did not speak highly of 'Communism' as he was a political person and was arrested and sent to a Russian jail. After his ordeal in a Russian jail he took mother, my two sisters, and myself and left Russia.

The war had just begun and we traveled in box cars and walked as much as we could on the Allied side. We were very fortunate as we ended up in West Germany. We lived in different towns for four years and my father worked for the American Army. He did not make much money, actually we were very poor. We lived in a one room shack with a blanket to cover the front door. It had a dirt floor and a pot belly stove in the middle of the room. Our heads were shaved to keep the lice at bay. We had a wooden bath tub and the toilet outside.

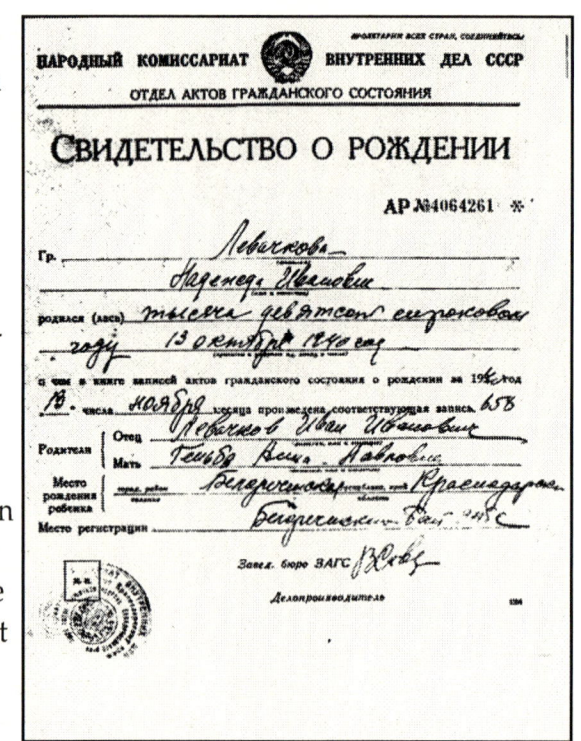

Nadia's birth certificate

(Continued on page 33)

CHAPTER THREE   CLASS BACKWARDS

(Continued from page 32)

The Americans were rebuilding Germany and in 1949, we were told we had to leave. The Americans told my father he had three options: he could either go to the USA, Canada or thirdly Australia. He chose the USA and we were to leave as soon as possible by ship to a sponsor in the USA. We were all very excited to go! Everyone in America was rich and it would be a new life for us all. We were very excited.

The voyage was very long ten days and I was very sick. The Red Cross had given us boxes with pencils and little things to play with on the voyage, but I was so sea sick I couldn't play with them. The Ocean was very rough in February and we had no medication for motion Sickness. It all stopped once we docked in Massachusetts Harbor on February 22, 1949. When we arrived we could not leave the boat as it was Washington's Birthday and everything was closed. We all looked at Boston with wonder from the deck of the boat!! My father said, "All the ladies in America had painted nails." We all giggled and could hardly wait to get off the boat. Can you imagine the excitement we felt arriving in the USA, knowing we were safe and would have a new life in a new country filled with many opportunities?

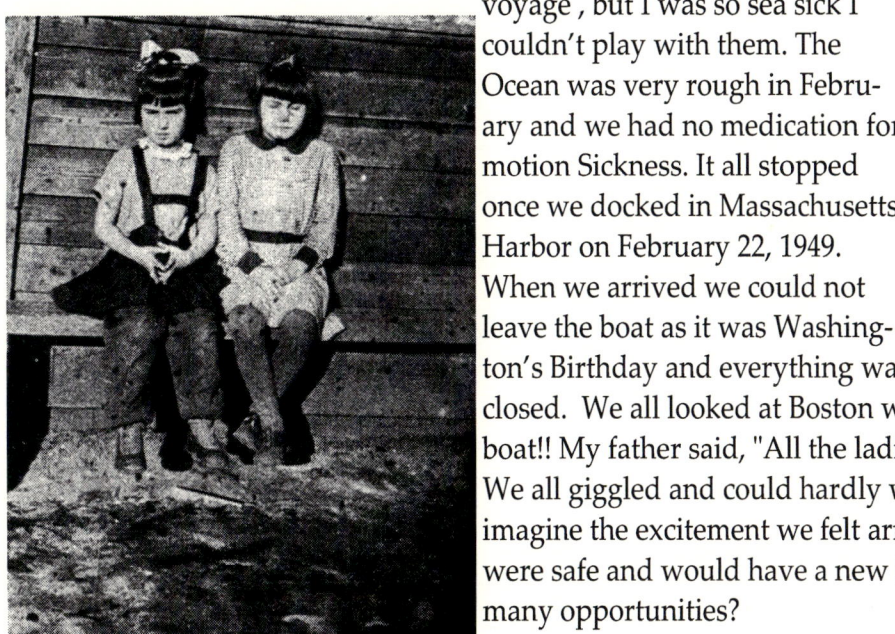

l to r Three sisters, Tamera, Helen & Nadia

l to r Nadia and Helen at camp in West Germany

(Continued on page 34)

(Continued from page 33)

We traveled from Indiana to the little town of Bloomington. We were met by the Family that sponsored us and everyone was excited for we were the first immigrants to come to this town. Our picture was in the paper and people donated many things to us like clothing and food. My Father was so pleased about this, as he had at that time only $25.00 in his pocket. We received a home in which to live. My father worked in the fields from sun-up to sun-down.

My father got ill towards the end of the year, as he was working too hard. He knew of some people who lived in Northeast Minneapolis. He contacted them and as soon as we could pay off our sponsor we moved to Minneapolis. We got an apartment across from Logan Park. I drew strength from my early years in Europe and living in Northeast Minneapolis. My roots were deep in both Europe and America. **Nadia Lewacko Yantos**

Nadia and family in front of "one room shack" in West Germany

CLASS BACKWARDS

CHAPTER FOUR:
ALL THIS AND HEAVEN TOO

The churches were all around us. Viewed from our young eyes, they were huge in stature. Their influence remained through our early years. We chose which one we should attend following our traditions. Families or some family members went to church, supported the church, played at the church, and in many cases were schooled there as well. There were so many of them in Northeast that many believed we made the Guinness Book of Records, being the only place in the country to have churches on all four corners of one block. Why so many in one section of the city? It was tied in with our heritage. In hindsight they were certainly the life-blood that held Northeast together. The following recollections reveal insights into church and religion in our early years, our holidays, and our future lives.

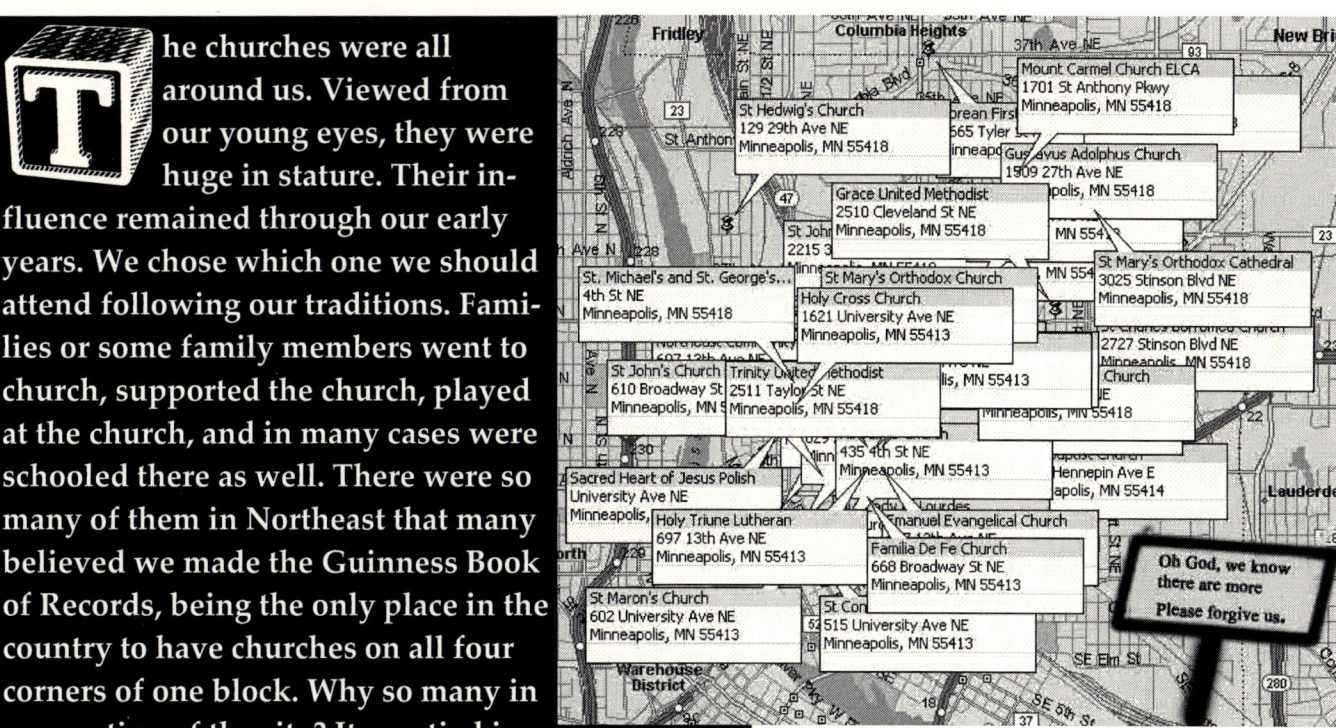

Ethnic Diversity — As our various descendants settled in Nordeast, they brought with them their languages and their churches. Late in the 20th century there were still a number of churches holding their worship services in the language of their ethnic origin. These churches were the source of close-knit communities and strong pride that we Nordeasters have in our area. I didn't recognize the religious diversity in our community until I was a young adult. I never realized that there were 14 Catholic churches in the area. With just a little research, and rest assured this was not exhaustive, I turned up five Baptist churches, one Episcopal church, eight Lutheran churches, three Methodist churches, two Orthodox churches, and one Presbyterian church. I can guarantee that I've missed another dozen or so. **Larry Kohout**

Catering to Nationalities — Is it any wonder that churches catered to their own nationalities? The Catholic churches built in the heart of the various ethnic settlements: The Irish-St Anthony, St. Boniface–the Germans, St. Cyril–the Slovakians, Holy Cross-the Polish, St. Hedwigs, All Saints, Our Lady of Lourdes-the French, St. Maron's-The Lebanese.
Rod Nelson

Lotsa Lutherans — There were numerous examples of ethnic diversity within the Lutheran churches at the time. From the '30s through mid '50s, there were about 20 Lutheran Synods, divisions organized along geographic lines and ethnic origins like three German, two or three Norwegian, one Swedish, Slovak, three or four Finnish, and more.
Bob Buntrock

Holy Cross Catholics —
A huge concentration of Polish people lived in N.E. Minneapolis. People who immigrated to America were sponsored by various churches or family members who arrived earlier. Holy Cross Church in N.E. sponsored a large number of Polish people and provided them with jobs. Many were hired by the Soo Line Railroad and were expected to live near the church so they could walk to church and to work. Some of the families were from the same town in Poland.

Records kept by churches before the '40s are the most accurate. Many births were at home. The midwife or aides would send the information months later to the city and it would not be totally true for dates. Death certificates were also more accurate in church records. **Claire Hudoba Rosenberger**

St. Johns Lutherans —
Since my ancestors were from northern Germany, we went to St. John's Evangelical Lutheran Church on Broadway and Washington. It was a Wisconsin synod church, formed originally in 1850 by Germans in Milwaukee with services conducted in German. I remember that each Sunday in those early years my mother would put 40 cents in the envelope for the collection. It seems like nothing now, but in those days moms didn't generally work. Only fathers worked outside the home. 40 cents was a sizable chunk for our family.

St. John's was a gray stone church, and I always thought it was a beautiful church, both outside and inside with its outside gothic features and beautiful dark woodwork inside. It also has striking stained glass windows. **Louie Paff**

St. John's Evangelical Lutheran Church

Confirmation in German — I grew up in lower N.E. across from Beltrami Park at Broadway and Fillmore. It was a very small well-defined area. Our neighborhood was mainly Italian and some Polish. Thus most everyone in my class was Catholic. They attended Our Lady of Mt. Caramel Church which was at the end of my block. I think it may have been the only church of any kind in our little neighborhood. Father Malley was the priest when I lived there and a long time beyond that. I remember my mom talking about attending St. Paul's Lutheran when they were young. It is on Lowry, west of Central Avenue. My grandparents lived on Quincy near the Soo Line. When they were young, she said that they had to learn their confirmation in German. I'm not sure how they accomplished that, but I know they thought it was really hard. **Sue Walker Mandery**

> CONFIRMATION CLASS
> IN GERMAN ONLY

Services At St. Paul's — My parents were German Lutheran immigrants to Nordeast. They came from small towns, in the early '30s, like so many others. Living in an apartment flat on Lowry, they began attending St. Paul's Lutheran Church, Quincy and Lowry, across the street. Until 1940, the year I was born, one service every Sunday was in German (one was in English.) Our pastor continued to preach a German sermon once a month on WCAL radio.
Bob Buntrock

Get Me To The Church On Time

As long as people lived near their church, it was easy to get there. Once they moved, however, it became more difficult. Streetcars or buses were not always the solution as their schedules changed on Sunday.

CHAPTER - FOUR   CLASS BACKWARDS

Complications—In the late '30s my family moved to our house up the hill (the only one they ever owned), on 19th between Garfield and Arthur. We continued to be members at St. Paul's Even though that was over a mile away This produced complications because Dad felt forced to sell his car ('37 Chevy) in 1942, mainly due to rationed tires rather than rationed gas. Living halfway between the Bryant-Johnson streetcar line and the Stinson Bus line gave us good transportation alternatives, but didn't do us much good for travel to church with Sunday schedules. Fortunately, neighbors on 19th kept their car and drove us to church. **Bob Buntrock**

The " Walk" — I've heard people say that if you were Catholic, or in some cases Lutheran, during the middle of the last century, you had to go to the church nearest to you. Well, at least for a while, that was true of those of us who grew up as Episcopalians in Nordeast. However, our nearest church was not a block away.

My father had sold his car after the war in order to raise money to buy a house on the corner of 32nd Avenue and McKinley Street. One of the reasons they felt comfortable in selling the car, I learned later, was that the new house was right on the Lowry bus line which, in addition to intersecting with two major downtown streetcar lines, ran right past our church. What Dad didn't know is that the bus only followed that route Monday through Friday. On Sunday, the route was abbreviated, ending at Lowry and McKinley – and only running once an hour. So from the time I was six and we moved into our new house, until I was about eight I have no memories of going to church at

St. Mathew's Episcopal Church
Lowry at the corner of Fillmore
Hennepin County Library, Special Collections

(Continued on page 40)

39

(Continued from page 39)

all. Turning eight, I all of a sudden started having to go to church with my Dad. Mom stayed home to take care of my two younger brothers.

I have virtually no memory of the church service. My Sunday memories are of the *walk* – let's call it a hike – from our house to the only Episcopal Church in Nordeast. A mile and a half may be no big deal for an adult, probably not even worth mentioning to a teen-ager, but to an eight-year-old that mile and a half was a marathon. I'm sure I remember taking 14 steps to every one step my father took. Also, my father never did anything by halves. When he set off to walk to church, *he walked.* I had to break into a run periodically to keep up with him. Our route carried us south on McKinley to what was then called the Brighton Cut Off, a street that cut diagonally southwest to intersect with Lowry. My Dad assured me that this was cutting several blocks from our walk. I was grateful for small favors. All the exercise put me in good shape to nap through most of the service. Following the service, I'd get a carton of juice and a donut which I considered to be fuel for the return walk. I can't tell you how I envied our neighbors who had to walk only three blocks to Saint Charles, the Roman Catholic Church for our neighborhood. Later in my life I converted.

Larry Kohout

Four Churches on one Block a world record?
Block bordered by 15th Ave on the north, Monroe St on the east, 13th Ave on the south, Madison on the west.

Crossing Bridges — In order to go to a Protestant church we had to go west on Broadway, over the Central bridge, and cross Logan Park. The church I went to was Emmanuel Lutheran. It was on a block that had a church on each corner.

Sue Walker Mandery

CHAPTER-FOUR — CLASS BACKWARDS

The Young And The Restless

We grew up learning highly valued religious principles. Our parents and grandparents brought to bear the importance they placed on religion. We were introduced to our church and all its rituals. We tried to behave. We really did. But we weren't always that successful.

Reformation — My first memories are of sitting with my parents throughout the services and being expected to stay quiet and behave throughout. There was no nursery for little kids. Being quiet and sitting still was difficult to do when I was small. When prayers were said everyone kneeled on the floor and turned around with their arms on the seat of the pew they'd been sitting on. No kneelers were provided in that church. During the kneeling I seized the chance to goof off a few times, such as rolling under the pew, which I thought was great fun. My parents didn't like that at all, and under threat of spankings, and I believe receiving one or two, I reformed my ways during prayers. **Louie Paff**

Escape — My first few years were at Notre Dame. Roger Monette and Jim Sarna went there also. I briefly attended one of the other Catholic schools, I think in first grade, but it was short-lived. I brought a water pistol to school and had it in my desk. I wasn't using it. But the nun saw it and took it away and I complained and so she hit me on my hands with the ruler. So I somehow climbed out the window in my classroom. The windows were wide open and they were on the ground floor. I went home and told my mom I didn't want to go back to that school anymore. My mom went to school and had a discussion with the nun and then changed me to Notre Dame. I don't think I was kicked out of Notre Dame. I transferred to Sheridan in fifth grade.
Wayne Mandery

Soaped — Church affairs, functions, and religious rites were very much part of our lives. We always said a table prayer and our bedtime prayers. As we grew older, we were on our own for prayers at bedtime. We were encouraged to join church functions, kid's groups, choirs, etc., and church attendance was mandatory (if healthy). We were to be on our best behavior, both at and away from church and bad language heard around the home was a cause for mouth washing with soap. We were admonished to heed our conscience on all aspects of behavior.
Bob Buntrock

Sit Still — The reverence and sanctity with which elderly neighbors attended church service certainly set the mood and the required etiquette on how to act and pray. They knew something I didn't. How to be holy! So you didn't look around, you tried not to cough or fidget, and you really thought about Jesus - or pretended to. **Rod Nelson**

Discovering Differences

Wannabe Catholic — I was a Norwegian Lutheran girl growing up in lower Northeast Minneapolis. The population of the area consisted of Polish Catholics, Russian Orthodox, Slovak and German Catholics. Needless to say, when it came to religion I felt out of place living in the neighborhood. My girlfriends

(Continued on page 43)

CHAPTER-FOUR — CLASS BACKWARDS

(Continued from page 42)

attended St. Cyril, St. Anthony and St. Boniface Catholic grade schools and churches. My friends made their first communion in their beautiful white dresses. I did so want to be Catholic! My mom, however, did make me a lovely light blue dotted Swiss with white ribbons on it, which I adored and that seemed to satisfy me.
Jean Torgerson Strong

Jean Torgerson in her light blue dotted Swiss

Religious Growth — Our Lady of Mount Caramel Church is the place where many of us Catholics received our First Communion (in our pure and innocent white clothing) and a few years later made our Confirmation. Religious growth at Our Lady of Mount Carmel was driven by Father Malley, but our population growth was driven by the Pope—remember the 14 McGuire kids and the 18 Yates kids? **Bob Peters**

Wasn't Everyone Catholic? — The thing I remember most about growing up Catholic was that I thought everyone in the whole world was Catholic. All my friends were, all the neighbors were, all my relatives were, and all the way to school I picked up Catholic kids. Why should I think there were other religions? It never entered my mind until I met some kids who went to Holland School and they weren't Catholic. I think I was in 6th, 7th, or 8th grade.
Patricia Godava Myslajek

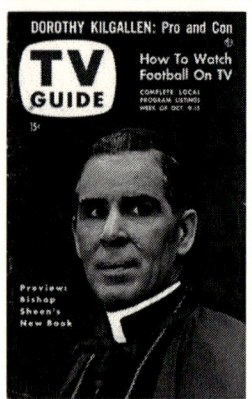

Bishop Sheen — When I was in third grade, my father had surgery for stomach cancer and began reading *The Power of Positive Thinking* to me. We also became big Sunday night fans of Bishop Sheen's TV program, so I thought of myself as sort of Catholic, not realizing what that meant. Sunday involved certain rituals. In the morning, our family drove 8 miles downtown to attend Hennepin Avenue Methodist Church. Before going to classes, I would sit with my parents at the beginning of the service and sing. My dad had a great booming voice and I loved the music. This would just take care of the beginning of the day. After church, we would have lunch at the Forum Cafeteria downtown and then go to a movie. The movies supplied much of my knowledge of the wrongdoings in the world. **Carol Lyons Larson**

Whatsit All About? — My idea of religion growing up in Northeast Minneapolis was an intriguing kind of passage. When I became aware of more buildings (churches) like the one I belonged to, I was puzzled. Why and what were these other churches all about? Why didn't my church like them and with so many around, why did we walk past some to get to ours? I don't recall ever learning about another person's faith until maybe I was 12 or so. I actually passed one Catholic Church – St Cyril's – on my way to our church at St. Anthony. At 6 or 7 years, I didn't know why, but with a strange name like St. Cyril's it seemed rather dark and ominous and I couldn't imagine who went there. Later I learned I should nod my head and say some few words when I passed it. I couldn't do it consistently, thought it kind of strange. As a teenager I began to hear of other churches around and some were not Catholic. I even joined a Boy Scout troop in a Lutheran church, but only once dared to go into the actual sanctuary. **Rod Nelson**

St Cyril and Methodius Church at 13th Ave NE and 2nd St.

CHAPTER-FOUR CLASS BACKWARDS

Mixed Marriage — My mother was Lutheran, my father Catholic. When they married, my father adopted Lutheranism. In my memory, there was no problem with this arrangement. They chose St. John's Lutheran Church on Broadway and Washington Street as our church. That became my religious home from age 3 until I was married there. **Carolyn Jodie Hagford**

Questions — I marveled at the large number of Catholic churches – with schools attached - that were within walking distance of my home. During one Lenten season, my neighbor Jimmy and his mother asked me to do the Stations of the Cross with them. Walking to 10 churches within a few hours (with time to pray at each one) was amazing. I lived one block from Holy Cross Church and School. I pondered some questions as I grew older. How could a church have a bowling alley in its basement? Didn't that make it un-holy? Why was it that the Catholic kids who prayed all day were the ones who threw rocks at me after school and who were the children I learned all my swear words from? I still haven't figured out the answers to those questions.
Carolyn Jodie Hagford

Growing Up Under the Influence

We attended Sunday School, Catechism, and later Confirmation classes for most of our religious instruction. Many of us attended parochial or Catholic schools. Up until the later 1940s, public schools set aside released time for religious training until it was declared unconstitutional by the Supreme Court. Some of us attended classes during the week as well. The lessons were etched in our young minds and in many ways continued to influence our lives much later.

Respect — When I received my own Bible in the fourth grade Sunday School class, our Pastor, Paul C. Dowidat took the time to *show* all of us how to correctly open a new Bible and how to treat it reverently. He was a formidable person to me in my younger years; I always averted my eyes when he walked by. It was not that I feared him, but rather respected him. **Carolyn Jodie Hagford**

CHAPTER - FOUR   CLASS BACKWARDS

Yes Your Holiness — I was enrolled in Sunday School in fourth grade or so. And for years after that I found that I had almost memorized the catechism that was used. I also was super thrilled to finally dress in the white trousers, shirt and tie to make my First Communion. It was the first big highlight of my young life. It was also a very proud moment for my parents. I recall how holy and special I felt walking down the aisle and then receiving the wafer that I hoped I wouldn't chew. Then I remained in Sunday School working on gaining all the knowledge necessary to be confirmed. Some of it was tough to remember or even make sense of – maybe we were allowed a little leniency on those parts. I can't remember any of it today. Confirmation involved the Archbishop from St. Paul coming and testing our knowledge in an oral setting. We recited well. Responded well with "Yes, your Holiness." And then somehow we were confirmed. And another proud moment for the family occurred. **Rod Nelson**

Rod in his communion clothes

Religious Fervor — I became a religious zealot in fifth grade. I believe it was due to a 'released time' program we had that allowed us during the middle of our school week to go to a church nearby for more religious training. Kathleen Coveney was my best friend in fifth grade and together we decided we were going to become disciples. We would walk home from school and warn any of the kids we ran into about the dangers of not believing in God. This lasted a few weeks until I started to preach to one of the students in our class, and he hit me in the stomach. There ended my religious fervor. Kathleen and I decided that being disciples was too dangerous, so we became detectives instead (another story). **Carol Lyons Larson**

CLASS BACKWARDS **CHAPTER - FOUR**

Gusto — Sunday school occurred before church in the church basement. The large room was partitioned off with portable wooden dividers for our classes. The chair backs slanted beyond the legs, and when I and some of the other boys were small we thought it was great fun to lean our chair backs against the wall and then sit down, thereby rocking the walls. Our teachers were not impressed, and I remember getting chewed out about it more than once. As we grew older we would sit in a different partitioned part of the room each year. Thinking back on having so many kids all in one basement, I bet it was really noisy. After the sessions with the teachers we would all gather together to have some announcements and to sing a few songs. The piano was an out of tune wreck, and the sweet old lady who played it never pressed all the keys at once - most every chord came out as an arpeggio. But we sang with gusto in spite of that. *Onward Christian Soldiers* was one of our favorites, and we sang it a lot.   **Louie Paff**

> **A**s we reached Junior High, many of us were confirmed in the religion we had followed in our younger years. Strict rules of conduct were to be obeyed. We had been given a clear and sometime strong or fearful message about what was "right" and what was "wrong." Still, we weren't always the best that we could be. Sometimes, our thinking was a little wayward.

No Lipstick — As we were confirmed, we were eligible for taking communion. In our strict Wisconsin Synod church, we had to express our desire to repent – silently – and submit a signed card at least one week before the monthly communion service. That way we could mull over our sins for many days be-

(Continued on page 49)

48

CHAPTER - FOUR CLASS BACKWARDS

(Continued from page 48)

fore we felt cleansed enough to receive the sacraments. Another stipulation was that girls could not wear lipstick, nail polish or head coverings as we went to the altar. That was Pastor Dowidat's decree, not God's, but I obeyed. This type of training became the basis for my obedient later years. I didn't know any better. Through this all, my church did not seem strict; it was what it was. I had schoolmates to interact with and none of them complained, so I just went with the flow. **Carolyn Jodie Hagford**

Running From Hell — As 13 year-olds, Denny and I were walking by St. Anthony Church mid-day mid week. I said let's go in. He had not been in a Catholic church and I had not been in one other than Mass or confession. So we were apprehensive as to what might happen. To make sure we didn't get caught, we crawled and sneaked our way from the back down to the front and we both barely made it out of the side door. I felt we were lucky for not being struck dead for such non-religious behavior. Once outside we ran from hell, I mean like hell. **Rod Nelson**

Authority — I remember how strict the nuns used to be when I went to junior high at Holy Cross. It wasn't all that bad for us though. We usually got what we deserved. One day in 8th grade, the priest, who usually taught our religion class was gone, so a nun, who usually took their break at that time, had to come in to substitute. Unfortunately, our class was getting rowdy. Two of the boys shot a peashooter at someone, and she thought it was Joey Godava and me. She had all of us go to two rooms to write "The Lord's Prayer" 100

(Continued on page 50)

times. Joey began each sentence with "Our Father which *aren't* in heaven…" The nun was very upset when she saw what he was doing and smacked his hand with a ruler. I couldn't help laughing. Then she turned around and slapped me in the face-hard enough to leave a mark.

In those days we went home for lunch. My cheek was still red, but I couldn't let my Ma see it. She would've been mad at me! So, I kept facing the other way and hid my red cheek in my hands. When I got back to school, it still was sort of red. When the Sister saw that, she really felt bad and apologized to me. I felt awful and told her I had it coming. We respected authority in those days. Nevertheless, she tried hard for the rest of the year to be good to me. Joey and I became her best pupils. **Jerry Kondrak**

Guilty — I attended St. John's (Wisconsin Synod) Lutheran Church which was a very strict Lutheran church. Of all the Lutheran churches, it was the strictest. All I remember about the church was the pastor was very serious and I always seemed to feel guilty about something, but I never knew quite what I was guilty for. It was not a happy church for me! They did, however, give all the children huge bags of candy and peanuts on Christmas Eve after the Christmas Program and that, of course, was supposed to make everything fine. **Jean Torgerson Strong**

Chapter Four — Class Backwards

No More Catechism

— I think I was in seventh or eighth grade when we had catechism class, and go on to confirmation. I think the class met once a week or so at church. Reverend Lystig, a rather severe Norwegian preacher, taught it. We had to memorized all these questions and responses. I think it was during that time that I started to question the whole religion and God thing, because it just didn't quite make sense to me. When I was younger, I took it seriously, because I remember one period when I was 9 or 10 when I decided I would read the whole Bible. I would read for a while every night before I went to bed. That must have gotten old fast, because I don't think I even got through Genesis. But Reverend Lystig took it all very seriously, and was very critical if we didn't know the right answers. There was a lot of guilt being promoted in that class, but I don't think I caught very much of it. It was not a happy class and I remember being really glad to get confirmed, knowing I wouldn't have to go back to catechism classes ever again.

Norman Solberg

Trinity Methodist Church Confirmation Class

St. Paul's Lutheran Confirmation Class

More Guilt — I usually had good Sunday school teachers who went past the lessons for the day and encouraged questions and discussion. Confirmation class was a little more rigid because Reverend Wilke was more old school and required extensive memorization of portions of Luther's Catechism, Bible verses, and the text of hymns. Reverend Lystig was a very nice man, but yes, a very strict Norwegian Pastor. Guilt is an awful thing and can be so paralyzing. Those days, "Hell and Damnation" was preached too easily. It would frighten me half to death! **Bob Buntrock**

No Big Deal — I attended confirmation class at Emanuel Lutheran Church by Logan Park, along with Diane Pearson and Barb Thayer. The only thing I remember is that we were told there would be a big oral test at the end and we were all really worried about that. It turned out to be no big deal at all and we all passed. **Sue Walker Mandery**

Going Astray — Our religious instruction had a different impact on each of us. Some of us have remained devout Christians and law abiding citizens all our lives. One ended up in prison, and no, it wasn't me :) I remember being shocked at the time - how could this guy who'd been through confirmation class do something bad enough to go to prison? **Carolyn Jodie Hagford**

Wine — For two years, between ages 11 and 13, a few of our Edison classmates (Denny Lindow, Judy McClure, Carolyn Jodie, Dale Farber, and I) were in confirmation class. The class was led by Pastor Dowidat, the man who built the congregation at St. John's and was the pastor there for 58 years. He was an awesome person who carried himself with perfect posture, gave excellent sermons, smoked cigars, and made the most outstanding tasting communion wine. He made it at home from a combination of domestic grapes and wild grapes that grew on his property on Long Lake. When Pastor Dowidat was 95 (he lived to 103), my wife and I visited him at his daughter's house. She dug up one of the few remaining bottles of wine and served it to us - it was as good as I had remembered. I really enjoyed Pastor Dowidat's sermons. I don't remember much of what he said, but I listened to him better than I have most preachers since.
Louie Paff

Luther League — Subsequent confirmation classes were much more active in both Lutheran League and Teen Choir as our social activities expanded to Christmas parties, and even a softball team. Luther League was fairly well established with older kids and we had a lot of fun in addition to more traditional church meetings. Once a month, we'd have a social with the big favorites bowling and even dancing at someone's house . Teen choir was also a social outlet. Who could ignore a night out (Wednesday) on a school night, sanctioned by parents, especially if you liked the music?   **Bob Buntrock**

Purgatory Sounds OK — I didn't go to a parochial school so I took catechism. Two things stuck in my mind: there were a lot of prayers to memorize and there were a lot of sins to avoid. Other than original sin, and mortal and venial sins, it seemed there were a bunch of other categories of sins. There were the seven or so *Deadly sins* and sins like gluttony and sloth etc. I figured my best bet was to try for purgatory – sounded like it would be a little boring but better than the alternative. **Dick Myslajek**

Dead People

Kozlak's Funeral Home — Every day I walked home from Holy Cross School to where I lived on 3rd Street near Lowry. I was usually with one of my classmates, and along the way we passed the Kozlak's Funeral Home on University. There were usually some dead people there. We thought, what better place did we have to pray for dead people, to get them out of purgatory faster, and to store up some heavenly points that we might need for ourselves after we died?

Kids normally shied away from funeral parlors, but Kozlak's was located about halfway home from school, and it offered a place to escape the cold weather or the heat. One of the employees was always near the door to greet visitors, and this made us feel welcome. To top it all off, we could get a paper cup of cool water from the big glass water dispenser that would bubble up and was such fun to use.

I felt most comfortable when Peter Kozlak was there to welcome us. He was always friendly and would escort us to the chapel to pay our respects. At the time,

(Continued on page 55)

(Continued from page 54)

I thought he was being very accommodating for us kids, but now I think he stayed with us just to keep us from getting into trouble. It was unlikely that we would have gotten into much trouble because as soon as we even thought about doing something wrong, the nuns would suddenly appear out of nowhere. Then we had to be on our super best behavior because we could always expect to get a poke from one of them along with a comment about what we should or should not have been doing.

Sometimes we would stop at Kozlak's and find that the same person was still there from the day before. Then we would say, "Hey, we already saw this lady!" but it didn't make any difference to us because we got to have our drink of water anyway.

I hope that all of those dead people eventually did get to heaven!
Janet Myrozka Mros

Funeral In the Parlor — When I was about 8 we lived next door to Grandma O'Rourke who lived in a two story house on 2nd and 14th Street. When she came outside , mother always talked with her over the fence covered with grape vines . I don't remember listening. But one day mother said we were going over there to her funeral. It was my first experience with death. The funeral parlor was actually in the living room of her home, a carry-over from the old days. The memory is still with me of walking into her front yard where we had seen and talked with her many times. Then we walked up her front stairs and into her living room to see lots of flowers

(Continued on page 56)

Grandma O'Rourke

(Continued from page 55)

and a coffin. I hadn't been to a funeral before and as we walked into the front room there were flowers everywhere. I had never seen so many flowers in a house. At the other side of the large room was an open casket. I could not really see into the coffin without standing on my tiptoes.

I was not sure at all what was going on except mother said she had died. I wonder how many other families had a wake in their homes at that time?

Rod Nelson

Religion was tied to our music, our holiday feasts, and our celebrations. As we grew older, it continued to play a role in many of our lives

Singing Hymns — As a child, I remember Christmas programs with gifts of popcorn balls, fruit, and a lot of singing. Of course. we were Lutheran! In fifth grade, my mother encouraged me to join the newly formed kid's choir. We sang maybe once a month at services plus in the Christmas program. Thanks to piano lessons starting at age 8, I've sung all four parts at sometime in my life.

Bob Buntrock

Rewards — Memories of my life within the circle of St. John's were many. One highlight was the Children's Christmas programs every Christmas Eve when we all raced to the basement after our performance to receive a paper bag of Christmas candy and a popcorn ball wrapped in cellophane. (I hated the popcorn ball.) In later years, my friend Pat and I played flute duets for the program. I remember walking to church and back home after Sunday school with my older sister, mostly without parents accompanying us. They were mainly Christmas and Easter attendees, but made sure that my sisters and I went every week. **Carolyn Jodie Hagford**

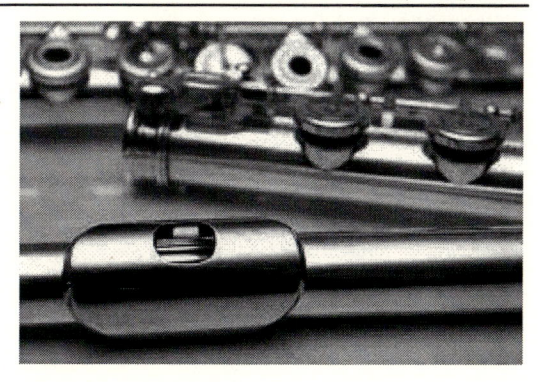

Fasting, Feasting — Religion, food, and tradition were a big part of celebrations and holidays. After we went through 40 days of lent, church services were held on Holy Thursday, Good Friday and Holy Saturday – baskets of food were blessed in church on Holy Saturday to be served with Easter Sunday dinner. After fasting during lent, midnight mass was often followed by a traditional Polish feast with family and friends including ham, kielbasa, hard boiled eggs, scalloped potatoes, Polish rye, poppy seed bread etc. And if not after midnight mass then for Sunday dinner. Christmas was celebrated in very much the same way. **Dick Myslajek**

57

Pascha Bread

Blessing the Baskets — The big holiday in our church was, and still is, Easter. It seemed to me that the Easter Holidays were like a Season of the year. Lent fasting and church services during the week began 40 days before Easter Sunday. No meat on Wednesdays or Fridays. Church services on Wednesdays and Fridays. Then we began the dairy free fasting the Wednesday prior to Easter. Mom made special unleavened bread (no eggs, milk, etc.). Also no butter on the bread! I think I lived on jelly sandwiches.

The highlight for us on Saturday was getting the Easter Basket ready to be blessed after the Midnight Service. Easter Saturday was baking homemade bread and a cooking marathon. Food in the basket was Pascha Bread (a round loaf of homemade white bread), butter in a glass container with a three-bar cross made out of little silver cake decorating beads. And more like, salt, ham, polish sausage, a round "cheese ball," and, of course, Easter eggs colored with intricate designs. Decorating the eggs was a highlight for us kids, and we got to do at least a couple of dozen of them since the holiday meals were always at my parents home and included all the relatives. **Penny Grivna Peters**

Louie's Pipe Organ

The Pipe Organ — When we sang hymns we often didn't sing all the verses. I loved the sound of the pipe organ in the church when I was young, and dreamed of having a castle with a pipe organ when I grew up. I have the pipe organ in my home, but it's not a castle. **Louie Paff**

A Future Nun

An occasional happening occurred on a large religious statue near my house as people were walking in front of it. People would come out of their houses and pin money to the statue. This only added to the mystique for me for the Catholic religion.

Being one of the few non-Catholics in my class, I was always very interested in the Catholic Church and all the traditions which I learned about from my friend Judy Chiodo. She took me for a visit into the church now and then to satisfy my curiosity. Little did we know that some day she would become a nun. **Sue Walker Mandery**

Weren't all Weddings Polish? Oom Pah Pah Oom Pah Pah...

Wedding Celebrations

Wedding celebrations are the one thing I miss the most about my Polish heritage. I regret that my nieces and nephews will never experience an old fashioned Polish wedding – especially the reception. No matter how expensive, there will never be a wedding reception that will ever come close. The wedding Mass was usually in the morning and the reception in the evening often at the PNA hall or church or another place such as the Knights of Columbus Hall... It consisted of a home cooked catered meal (often by a small local caterer) —chicken and polish sausage, mashed potatoes, vegetable, maybe sauerkraut, bread and of

Wedding Photos from the Sharon Matt Collection

(Continued on page 60)

(Continued from page 59)
course cake from a local bakery— followed by a polka dance. There were many small local polka bands. And, of course drinks for all – usually a free bar, tended by uncles and friends. What made it special was the Polish music—not only polkas but old-fashioned waltzes, schottisches, and mazurkas by a live band that could be enjoyed by young and old alike. That's what you expected and that's what you got; and no one was disappointed and most everyone stayed till the end. The celebration continued into Sunday where family and friends assembled for the opening of the gifts and left-over food.
Patricia Godava Myslajek (class of 1960)

Wedding Photos from the Sharon Matt Collection

A New World — I never knew people danced at weddings until later in life when I was invited to my friends' family weddings. I was astounded that they did that. **Carol Lyons Larson**

Shivaree — Some families rented a hall for a wedding dinner and dance. We lived on 2nd across from the ODHS hall as we called it. On Saturday nights, kids in our block would go over to the stairs in front and bang on pots and pans until the groom came out and threw money, a real shivaree – lots of loose change. We scrambled – you had to be aggressive - for whatever coins we could pick up and then ran home. Sometimes we dared to go back a second time. At the PNA hall on 13th Ave, we had to wait on the sidewalk pounding our pans until someone went upstairs to get the groom. It was a long flight of stairs that he threw the coins down – harder to get at, but we did. **Rod Nelson**

No Kissing — I was married at St. John's, and we had our dinner reception for 150 in the basement. It was the thing to do for a strict Wisconsin Synod wedding. Even then the Church set the rules, my new husband and I could not kiss at the altar during the ceremony. We got around that by racing up the aisle and having a clincher in the narthex. **Carolyn Jodie Hagford**

Final Writes

Faith — For me, my years at St. John's laid a ground work of religious faith that has lasted throughout my life. I feel blessed to have had such a good religious upbringing. **Louie Paff**

An Angelic Louie Paff

An Angelic Bob Buntrock

Influences — I definitely had a more conservative church upbringing than I've experienced since then, but I treasure those times and that background. The encouragement (and yes, prodding) of my family, parents and sister, were powerful influences in my life, and not just my church life. **Bob Buntrock**

CLASS BACKWARDS

CHAPTER-FOUR

CHAPTER FIVE:
OUR NEIGHBORHOODS

In our early years, our lives were centered on our families and our neighborhoods. We rarely moved to a different house and if so, not very far. Often relatives lived on the same block. We felt like everyone on our block was related! While we were school-age, we were safe and free to go outside on our own. At first, it was a front yard, a back yard, down the block on this side of the street only, eventually to maybe crossing the street - all within vocal calling distance of our home. As we grew older we were free to explore the blocks around us.

This was one of the things that made Northeast Minneapolis unique. It was like a small town. The people we saw outside of our immediate families eventually took on personalities as we aged and became like an extended family. Each neighborhood had an identity: "Dogtown" "The Valley" "The Hill" "The Quarry" just to name a few.

Walk with us as we head back to our homes, streets, and neighborhoods. Many familiar places – slightly changed – still remain.

On the left—L to R Dale Halverson, Jim Terry, Dick Myslajek, Gary Pierson , Dodd Knutsen, Owen Green, Dennis Terry, Mickey Graham

L to R Karen Kleshold ,Rod Nelson, Jean Torgerson

Front row - L to R Tom Scales, Tom Graham, Betty Kay Neeb , Ted Lukaska, Lynn Knutsen, Mickey Graham, John Scales   Back row - l to r Dodd Knutsen, Dick Myslajek, Carol Bender, Jim Terry, Dale Halverson, Dennis Terry

CLASS BACKWARDS — CHAPTER - FIVE

Roller Skating in An Exciting World — Until I was thirteen years old, I lived three houses down from Mike's Bar on 4th Street and 15th Avenue. That intersection was a lively place. Across the street from Mike's was Johnson's Bar. Not as raucous as Mike's – it must have had a gentler clientele. I would put my on roller skates and bring my roller skate key in case I had to tighten them, and go to the corner to skate. The sidewalk was made of those large blocks of concrete and was quite smooth. In front of my house and along the fronts of the other houses, the sidewalk consisted of small blocks and was very bumpy where the tree roots had won the battle between manmade and nature.

Sometimes happy men would come out of Mike's and give me a nickel. Wow! Now I could buy a Nut Goodie candy bar at Rolig's Drug Store on 4th Street and 13th. What a treat!

 I recall a time roller-skating on the corner when I stopped to watch a deliveryman. He had the metal door in the sidewalk open and was delivering under Mike's Bar some huge metal barrels filled with a mysterious elixir that would make the customers happy. He asked me if I wanted a taste from one of them and I nodded my head. What he squirted in my mouth from a tube was bubbly, cold seltzer. I felt very lucky to get that taste – free.   **Carolyn Jodie Hagford**

CHAPTER - FIVE CLASS BACKWARDS

Dogtown — Dogtown was a closely-knit neighborhood bordered by Broadway on the North and by Central Avenue on the West. The South border was Spring Street and the East border was Johnson Street. Settled in the '20s and '30s by Italian immigrants, the term *Dogtown* came about because no one wanted to use the slur name "Dago" used to identify Italian people. This was the neighborhood I grew up in.

The Bug House (Margaret Barry House) was the neighborhood magnet where my friends and I all learned to get along. Beltrami Park and its Park Board Sports Programs brought us into contact with kids outside of *Dogtown* from Logan, and other kids from the Nut House. We used the alleys and backyards to play tag, hide and go seek, or kick the can until it got dark most summer nights, feeling safe and secure.

Everyone knew every family. On Saturdays, we rode our bikes or walked to the Saturday matinees at the *Princess, Arion* or *Hollywood* Theaters. We earned money for this by working on truck farms or delivering newspapers. We also collected pop bottles and turned them in for pennies to the corner grocery stores, Delmonico's, Spano's, Rusciano's and Schullo's, to buy popsicles.

During our single digit years we discovered *Dogtown*. During our double digit age we explored *Dogtown*. They are cherished memories and, more important, they are "Nordeast" memories.
Bob Peters

Margaret Barry House 759 Pierce Street

Looks like hide & seek

Delmonico's Italian Foods

65

Bob Buntrock's House on 19th Ave.
The Place I Will Always Call Home

Fritz Adler (Grounds Keeper) Feeding the Salvation Army Camp Deer
Courtesy of
Hennepin County Library, Special Collections

The Place I Will Always Call Home — I grew up in a small bungalow typical in the neighborhood, on 19th Avenue N.E., between Garfield and Arthur Streets. I believe the neighborhood was built in the '20s. When my parents and sister moved in 1937, that house was the first and only house they ever owned. I told my folks that when I grew up, I'd move back in and live there myself.

Four of us lived in that one-story, two bedroom bungalow. When World War II was over, Dad decided it was time to remodel and get more space. He and friends finished off the attic, creating two rooms under the eaves with storage space where the ceiling got too low.

With all of its disadvantages, small kitchen, small rooms, creaking stairs, I loved that house. I left at age 20 to get married and move into an upper duplex a mile away, never to live there again. When Dad died, it was a wistful experience to sell the house to perfect strangers, probably completing the turnover of the neighborhood I grew up in, 30-50 years before. **Bob Buntrock**

Living On the Edge of Northeast Minneapolis — We lived at 29th and McKinley Street, one block East of Stinson Blvd. and literally the end of the city. There were open fields, and farms to the east. We used to play ball on a triangle of land on 30th and Stinson Blvd. I thought it was

(Continued on page 67)

(Continued from page 66)

a huge piece of land...well it was to a ten year old. I don't remember teams, or even scores in the games, just waiting for my turn to bat and hoping I could hit it a long ways. Two or three of us would walk following Stinson Blvd. north one mile to the Salvation Army Camp. If we went in the spring, before any activity there, we could play by Silver Lake catching snakes, frogs, and looking in the cabins. It was very exciting, especially if we did not get caught.

When construction did come in the early fifties, we would go explore the new houses being built. It was so fun to walk through the rooms especially when just the studs were put up. This was strictly a not allowed activity both by parents and the builders. We did get caught and warned to stay away, but it was so much fun!
Kathleen Coveney Fields

Salvation Army Camp Goats with Fritz Adler (Grounds Keepter) Courtesy of Hennepin County Library, Special Collections

All In The Family — We lived in the Valley as I was growing up. Many of my relatives lived there too. My dad was a butcher and owned the Larson Brothers' Meat Market on Johnson Street employing his brother Ray. My Uncle Jack Dusenka, married to my aunt, Anna Semanko, leased a bar from Kozlak's and called it Jax Café. As the story goes, when Uncle Jack went to get the sign made, the painter in Northeast Minneapolis suggested spelling it

(Continued on page 68)

(Continued from page 67)

'Jax' for the notoriety.

Jack Reshetar, who lived two blocks away from our duplex, was smaller in stature than my Uncle Jack, and when he opened a bar, it became known as Little Jack's.

Later, in 1948, my dad and four other men formed the beginnings of what later became the Northeast State Bank. In 1950, I officially became a Hill kid and moved up to 31st and Buchanan. Our new house was a four-bedroom white rambler with a spacious yard, much different than the duplex in The Valley. **David Larson**

Little Sisters of the Poor — As young playmates, Jean Torgerson and I grew up with the huge brick wall of the Little Sisters of the Poor that almost completely surrounded our block. The wall was capped off with high wrought-iron fencing that made it even more intimidating. Our small corner where we lived was the only section with houses on it. What was beyond the wall seemed like a secret garden to us. Lilacs were always tempting, protruding out from the fences on the wall so during early summer all of us kids would climb the fence and pick bouquets for our moms. We knew we shouldn't do it, but kids will be kids. The man who took care of the yard would get after us and then we would get down. He

*Wall outside the
Little Sisters of The Poor
On Broadway between 2nd & 3rd Ave.*

(Continued on page 69)

CHAPTER - FIVE　　　　　　　　　　CLASS BACKWARDS

Child in front of
Little Sisters Wall
circ 1945

(Continued from page 68)

must have been the same man that chased out anyone who climbed over to get a ball. I think we enjoyed the challenge of the climb as well. These ventures over the wall must have been where we got stories of burials and old mean people. We were always trying to see over it, but we were too short. Even today driving by it is somewhat amusing thinking about pulling ourselves up by our fingers on the lower sections to peek on the other side. Only recently, while sharing our stories, did we find out that while we feared what was beyond the walls, another classmate related how she would enter on the other side via the large gate and stairway to visit elderly people being cared for in it. As kids we were not aware of what other kids were experiencing. The "Little Sisters of the Poor" is on the National Register of Historic Places in Minnesota. **Jean Torgerson Strong and Rod Nelson**

House in the Valley

A Pysanky Egg

*House on the Hill
32nd & McKinley
(from back)*

The Valley Versus the Hill — In spite of the fact that all of Nordeast was considered our home, there were differences existing between the Valley and The Hill that we weren't aware of until we grew older. The Valley folks carried with them more 'Old World' culture. I remember feeling a certain amount of envy/resentment of people from The Hill when I spent my first ten years of school at Sheridan living N.E. at 6th Avenue and 4th Street. Sheridan drew students from lower N.E. There was a certain amount of homogeneity to The Valley. It was more of an industrial area. My dad was a laborer, and I imagined that people on the hill were snobbish, but as I grew up and my family moved into a duplex on Taylor Street near 22nd, I realized that there were nice people from all areas. Looking back, it was silly, but at the time it was important to me. I grew to appreciate the great diversity of people I met. I think back about the mother in the Ukrainian family next door who gave me a beautiful pysanky egg each Easter. I still have them. Nordeast Minneapolis was a fabulous place to grow up and experience life. We took good care of our homes and yards. There was a sense of pride in both. **Louie Paff**

Old World Culture — It was a generalization, but the folks on The Hill seemed more reserved white collar workers as compared to the many blue collar workers living in The Valley. I loved both areas, but I enjoyed The Valley more. There was just more of a European atmosphere living in lower Nordeast. Our

(Continued on page 71)

CHAPTER - FIVE   CLASS BACKWARDS

(Continued from page 70)

neighborhood was a very Polish, Russian and Slovak neighborhood. They had many Old World ways and they were predominantly Catholic.

Needless to say, I sometimes felt kind out of place being the only Norwegian Lutheran girl living there. In the summer time, the Ragman would come into our neighborhood looking for rags. He usually came three or four times a summer. He looked liked a gypsy and had a horse that pulled his wagon. Actually, he was rather scary to me.

The Gypsy?

My early years growing-up in the forties from 1940 through 1950 in Northeast Minneapolis were spent on 12th Avenue and 3rd Street. I lived in two different houses on 12th Avenue.

The first house was the upstairs of a duplex. Our landlady, Mrs. Ganzer, a retired nurse and a very kind woman, had a big fluffy dog, which I adored. The dog was very tolerant of me as I tried to get as close to her as possible. I practically sat on her.

Mrs. Ganzer had a chicken coop in her backyard with a rooster or two and quite a few hens that produced wonderful eggs. You didn't see many chicken coops in the city at that time.

When I was three years old, we moved down the block and moved into the lower level of a duplex. In 1950, my folks be-

(Continued on page 72)

Jean Torgerson and the Dog

gan looking for a house to purchase and they finally found the house on 19th and Pierce Street, which they moved into in April of 1951. It was a very traumatic move for me, as I had to leave my friends in Lower Northeast. Being an only child I had plenty of time to worry about this move. As it turned out, I worried for nothing. **Jean Torgerson Strong**

The Ragman and Gypsies — The ragman would come down the street in his horse drawn open cart. He would collect rags saved by families. But we never really had any so I only watched him park and pick up a few here and there. Nothing was said by either as we just kept our distance and looked at the only horse drawn cart to come down the streets.

The Ragman

The Gypsies (maybe just neighbors moving) came into town or down the street every so often. At least that's what mother called them. We were warned to stay in the yard or house. All we saw were some old cars and some wagons. A very short parade. Don't know where they came from or where they were going. Never found out, but I was hesitant to be on the street when they came by. **Rod Nelson**

A Lesson Learned For a Lifetime —
When our family lived on the hill at 32nd and McKinley Street while it was not at all unusual in the summertime to see horse drawn weed cutters and even a horse drawn milk wagon, I'd never seen a ragman. Then, on one of those marvelous summer days when the sky was clear and blue except for a few high flying clouds, I heard a noise I'd never heard before. It was a whole herd of my friends and other neighbor kids all yelling and singing out. As they got closer I began to understand some of what they were yelling. I kept hearing the word ragman, though I wasn't at all sure what that was. I was also hearing the word "sheeny."

I finally realized that the noise was coming from the alley south of 32nd Avenue. I ran to the alley and saw a horse drawn wagon coming slowly down the alley surrounded by all these kids running along and yelling that the ragman, or sometimes that the "sheeny," was coming.

I ran into the house to tell my mother that the sheeny was coming, only to face a swift explosion from my mother. To my ten year old innocent mind, there were no derogatory terms. My mother gave me a swift education. While I somehow always knew that you did not use the "N" word for a black person, my mother taught me that there were a number of the other words that were offensive. She said these words were never to be used in any kind of company, polite or oth-

Horse Drawn Dairy Wagon
Courtesy of Hennepin County Library
Special Collections

(Continued on page 74)

(Continued from page 73)

erwise. Somehow, her mostly Germanic mind would never tolerate Polish jokes or other stories that stigmatized any particular group.

Good going Mom.   **Larry Kohout**

Dick Myslajek's House on the Hill

Our Neighborhood on the Hill — Our family moved into a newly built home on 3214 Pierce Street N.E. when I was about two or three (1942/1943). Although it was well within a mile of the city limits, our block and many of the surrounding blocks were almost half empty lots—providing many interesting playground areas which the kids in neighborhood took advantages of.

With some exceptions, most of the homes on our block and in the immediate area were new or recently built - it was the newest area of N.E. but had one of the oldest schools in the city - Edith Cavell on 34th Ave and Pierce Street. Our lot was on the N.E. side of Norwegian Hill, one of the highest spots within the city limits. Our area was called Oak Hill and was dominated by oak trees before development.

I'll admit I didn't come fully aware of the neighborhood until I was six or eight years old. Most of the families were of about the same age demographically and we had plenty of playmates—almost all boys of approximately the same age. My world ran on both sides of Pierce Street from the

(Continued on page 75)

(Continued from page 74)

corner of 32nd Avenue down half a block north.

I can still remember the names of the families and naturally of my playmates, like Dodd Knutson, Dale Halverson, and Jim Terry.   **Dick Myslajek**

The Hill: Illusions of Sameness and Stability —

I lived in a moderately small stucco house on 28th and Arthur Street in Northeast Minneapolis. Growing up, I never wanted to live anywhere else. In the summer I would savor the smell of freshly mown lawns and in the fall, heaps of leaves burning by the curb.

If you took a picture of our neighborhood, you would see a deceptive sameness to it. Mostly three-bedroom stucco houses, with well-kept grassy lawns and 50-foot elderly elm trees bordering clean sidewalks. Our house was on the corner lot framed by three small hedges. My best friend, Audrey Kitoski, lived next door in an identical house. Our friend Elsa Zinter lived next door to her in a house that stood out from the other houses, with white siding and an arbor in the backyard.

We were proud of our middle class standards of the '40s and lived within our means, being one-car families and only having one of our parents (our dads) work at a job outside of the

When We Still Had Elms

(Continued on page 76)

(Continued from page 75)

house. That's what we shared. But if you looked closely, we were different too. Elsa's dad was a doctor, Audrey's dad drove a Blackey's Bakery truck, and my dad was a judge. There were differences in our heritage, and our religions: Elsa's parents were German and she went to a Lutheran church; Audrey's parents were Polish and her family was Catholic; I was confused about my nationality and I was Methodist. I was told I was mostly Scotch by my mother, but after my parents passed away, I found out I was half-Irish from a relative of my dad's who did a genealogical study. Of course, my perceptions, just like the stucco on our house, aged and cracked with time. I would learn, as I grew older, that our neighborhood was not as stable and safe as I once believed. There were some troubled families, and even a suicide. The hardy Elms gradually became diseased and had to be removed. But my reality when I was a child was that I grew up in a kind, well-ordered place. I believed all people were good and the elm trees would never go away.

Carol Lyons Larson

Carol Lyons Larson Home of Stability

CHAPTER-FIVE CLASS BACKWARDS

The Quarry — A place on interest to me is located near 18th & Johnson Street N.E. The reason for the interest is that our family from 1945 to 1947 lived on the adjoining property of the North Star Concrete Co. which backed up to the Quarry Pit. My father was the foreman of the North Star business and was in charge of the operation of making huge concrete culverts which were used throughout the city.

I remember, as children, my sister and I played Hide and Seek and imaginative games in the round culverts that were stacked everywhere in the cement yard. It was always a thrill as a kid to watch the trains go in and out of the area filled with sand, gravel, and rock. Of course, we were never allowed to go near the Quarry. There was large equipment used to dig, crush, and move the rock and a waterhole at the bottom of the pit presented dangerous conditions to anyone wandering into that area. We heard stories of kids actually swimming in the waterhole.

Marilyn Sexton Sitting on the Culverts in the North Star Company Yard

After the concrete company closed, we moved from that location in 1947. In later years there was blasting of the rock in the quarry and after that for many years the entire pit was filled in with debris. Today, on the entire property where the pit and the North Star Company was located, stands the Quarry Shopping Center.
Marilyn Sexton Lubrecht

CLASS BACKWARDS — CHAPTER-FIVE

CHAPTER SIX:
HAPPY DAZE

We made do with cramped spaces…Nooks and crannies helped. Coal furnaces and wood-burning stoves warmed our houses. We saved water for Saturday night baths and sometimes we shared the bathwater. Our mothers mended our clothes and darned holes in socks. None of this felt like hardship. It was the way life was.

There were advantages to that life. Our food was freshly grown. We had victory gardens and raised chickens for food. And when we needed ice or cold milk, it was delivered to our doors. We relied on neighborhood markets and corner stores. Meal times were special because we had time to eat together and talk about our day. Hard work was valued and we had chores to do around the house. In retrospect, it was a good way to live.

A Northeast Four-Plex

Our Homes, Inside Out

Apartment Living — My parents and I lived in a second floor apartment in a four-plex on N.E. 6th Avenue near 4th Street. Life was very simple in those days, but also very

(Continued on page 80)

(Continued from page 79)

good. My father worked and my mom stayed home .

Our apartment had one bedroom and a little den with no door. My space was, of course, the den. A curtain could be pulled part way across the opening to give me some semblance of privacy. I had a hideaway bed in there. There was little space for anything else. Hooks on the wall at the foot end of the bed held some of my clothing. Wooden peach crates held the rest.

By the time I was 12, I was tall enough so that if I stretched out on my bed I could touch all four walls at once. The kitchen had cabinets that were painted white, and one lower door tilted outwards. I learned that it was a flour bin. We had an old fashioned gas stove with burners that had to be lit by matches every time, and an oven on the side.

In the hallway behind the kitchen was a pantry where food supplies were kept. I had a favorite item in that pantry, a big Nash's Coffee jar that held brown sugar. Many times when mom wasn't around, I'd open that door and eat a lump of brown sugar—it was sooo good. I'm sure my mom knew I was taking brown sugar but she never said anything about it. **Louie Paff**

This Old House — After our house was remodeled, my sister got the front room, which meant that I got her room downstairs in the back of the house. A bed was also placed in the back upstairs room, which was a guest room and where my maternal grandmother stayed with us during the winter (summers, she stayed with her other daughter on their farm up north

(Continued on page 81)

(Continued from page 80)

near Duluth). Other improvements included converting the coal furnace to natural gas and installing a real gas water heater along side. This was a real luxury because prior to that, Dad would fire up a coil water pipe heater to get enough hot water for Saturday night baths. Before the conversion, I remember Dad stoking the furnace for the night and since he was up early anyway, stoking it again in the morning for the day.

I also remember deliveries of coal down the chute into the coal bin at the rear of the basement. Afterward, we kept the unused coal bin for a storage room. It was a convection furnace, with that gigantic octopus of piping to distribute the heat throughout the house.

We kept that system which worked quite nicely in a small house. There was even a pipe, which ran to the upstairs through the back of my folks' bedroom closet. Because of the direct flow of heat, that front bedroom had more than enough heat and usually had to be turned down to avoid roasting. **Bob Buntrock**

Octopus Forced Air Furnace

Shoveling Coal

The Semanko & Larson Duplex

Sharing a Duplex — We lived in the upper level of a two bedroom red brick duplex on 24th and University Avenue. My Uncle Peter Semanko and his wife, Mary, lived on the lower level. There were four boys in our family, and as the family grew, a rollaway was needed in the dining room. We added on a stucco porch and sometimes it was warm enough, that's where Glenn and I slept. We would take a bath on Saturday night, often sharing the bath water due to wartime restrictions. **David Larson**

The Bungalow — Our house was small by today's standards, but was a typical two bedroom middle class bungalow of the time and similar to many of the homes on our block and in the area. Some homes had finished attics but very few if any had finished basements. We never had a garage while we lived there but most of the neighbors had garages or had them built in the late '40s-early '50s. Garages were unattached, accessed from the alley and single car. Many families on our block didn't have a car at that time. Our house was built on a then standard 40 foot city lot (about 100 feet deep) with a paved public sidewalk, a grass boulevard eventually planted with maples and an unpaved cinder covered alley (to provide winter traction), which was unforgiving if you fell down on the cinders. The alley was

(Continued on page 83)

(Continued from page 82)

eventually paved with concrete, which was an event that was watched by all of the kids in the neighborhood as it progressed.

To this day, I remember one of the dump truck drivers because we all thought he looked like Bob Hope. The streets in the area were fairly stable, not paved but consisted of some kind of base material (maybe regular dirt) covered with a layer of tar. Every few years the city would come and turn up the street, roll it with a big roller, and finally cover it with tar and sand. The kids on the block also considered this an event, but my mom was concerned about my tracking in tar on my shoes and for a while, I had to take them off before I came in the house. **Dick Myslajek**

Street grading—one of summer's excitements

Quonset Huts — I remember asking my parents about the Quonset huts located on Buchanan Street just outside of the Quarry. I learned that after World War II, Quonset huts were developed from prefabricated corrugated steel and plywood ends. They were much needed temporary housing for returning veterans and married students. Divided in the middle, one family lived in each end. They had a living room, 2 bedrooms, kitchen, and a bath. Heated with fuel oil (tank outside of each building) they were cold in the winter and unbearably hot in the summer. **Carol Lyons Larson**

Quonset Huts at 1500 Buchanan St. Northeast, Minneapolis, 1946. Image courtesy of the Minnesota Historical Society

Food for the Gods and she was paid by the devils.

Every Dollar Counted — My grandmother, who lived at 611 Broadway, was creative at making money to support her family. She was of modest means but made up for it with hard work. As a way of earning money, she washed curtains from other households in her kitchen, cooking them in the cooker to whiten them and placing them on stretchers to dry with no wrinkles. She also baked homemade angel food cakes for "the rich people." The cakes were made with fresh eggs, which she whipped by hand. Frosted with cherry icing, they were beautiful and delicious. The sound of her stirring the frosting in the blue enameled bowl is still vivid to me. She rarely was paid more than $2 for a cake, but every dollar counted.
Mary Kranak Cheleen

Johnny Cakes — I've loved to eat so I have fond memories of food. My mother was a good cook as were many of our friends and relatives. One favorite food was "Johnny Cake" cornbread baked in a square pan and served with maple syrup.

My Dad was a letter carrier and left for work early so the only breakfast I ever ate with him were on Sundays or Holidays. We had traditional Sunday noontime dinners. One favorite was homemade chicken soup, with leftover chicken (including the bones), carrots, celery, and homemade egg noodles. When my maternal grandmother lived with us in the winter, she'd roll out the dough on the breadboard, and cut them freehand into strips. I still remember those rich, irregular noodles and that great, rich soup. Sunday suppers were less elaborate.
Bob Buntrock

Johnny cakes — buttered - the heathens

Pork Hocks — German attributes affected food choices. Thus, meat and potatoes were strong in my family. A favorite dish my mom would make was pork hocks and dumplings cooked with sauerkraut. Every Sunday dinner (at midday), we had a beef roast with potatoes, carrots, and onions, and we always had it after we got home from church. My mom also insisted that we have a yellow vegetable and a green vegetable at every main meal, so that helped balance the menus.
Louie Paff

With beans you could find both yellow (wax) and green in the same vegetable

Neighborhood Markets

We grew up with small stores within walking distance, providing exercise, variety, and daily contact with our neighbors. They became meeting places, and sometimes, if our family couldn't afford the bill, we would be given "credit" and allowed to pay later.

Second Street Market — I don't think my mom, my sister, or I ate anything until I was about 4 or 5. To my knowledge, at that time, Mom never shopped for food and Dad was away from home and then away being in the service. We lived on 12th Ave. just up from 2nd St. The Second Street Market and Meat Market was just down the block. At an age of 5 or 6, I was sent to the meat market for wieners and hamburger. I loved the

(Continued on page 86)

(Continued from page 85)

sawdust on the floor, but didn't know why it was there until later. Many months passed and the new owner would let me sprinkle out new sawdust. It was in this market I saw my first dial phone. Don't know who I called, but I got to climb up on the stool in the glass enclosed office by the counter and play with it. It seemed no matter how many digits I dialed, it rang, so I'd hang up. I recall feeling pretty successful. **Rod Nelson**

Do you remember? They really did look like this.

Engleson's — We bought groceries from neighborhood stores and carried them home. The place where my family usually shopped was Engleson's, on the corner of 6th Avenue and 5th Street. I loved the long-handled tool with which boxes of cereal were plucked off high shelves. I also loved going for Popsicles on a hot summer day. One day I bought a can of pressurized whipped cream, and gorged myself on it. It tasted so good! We seldom ate out. **Bob Buntrock**

Brix — Brix grocery store was on another corner. It was an interesting place filled with interesting things. My mother could send me to get a quick purchase; maybe flour or apples or something she needed to finish making dinner. The grocer used long-handled poles to get the boxes down from the higher shelves. Being in that store was like going to a circus, seeing the grocer grabbing the box you wanted and bringing it down to my arms. **Carolyn Jodie Hagford**

Basements

Monster From the Basement—The basement was a scary place when I was little. A big oil furnace that heated water for the radiator heating system sat in the middle of the floor. During the winter, it made fierce rumbles that made me think it was going to blow up and I was really afraid of it. In 2008, I visited the caretaker of the four-plex and he gave me a tour. In the basement, I saw a really tiny gas furnace. I remarked on it and the old oil furnace and how it scared me when I was small. He said that same furnace scared him too, and he'd gotten the landlord to replace it just the year before, in 2007. It made me feel better knowing an adult was afraid of that furnace too. **Louie Paff**

One of the Monsters

Coal Truck Ready to Deliver a Season's Worth of Coal (Photo courtesy of www.fidelitybs.com)

Stoking the Furnace—Our original furnace was coal-fired. My dad had to shovel in coal in the a.m. and p.m. We had a coal bin in the basement with a small metal-hinged door at the back of the house. Coal was delivered by a large truck - usually in the fall before the heating season. I remember one year the ground must have been soft from rain because there was a long rut in our lawn from the alley to the house made by the delivery truck. Shortly thereafter, we converted to natural gas. **Dick Myslajek**

Combination wood burning and gas stove

Saturday Night at the Tub

Little Things That Made a House a Home

Splish-Splash—Luckily, I grew up to bathe myself. We used to bathe standing in front of the kitchen sink using a washbasin while Mom cleaned my younger siblings and me. Our first two apartments had only a bathroom stool. Our first home the same. But at least we had a large gas and wood-burning stove that would be stoked up with large pots of water on it to be heated for our Saturday baths. Papers were spread on the floor and set in front of the stove for heat while we took our turns sitting in a large galvanized washtub. Little ones first, then finally myself. I usually got some additional hot water added. Don't remember how we ever did drain it. Maybe out the backdoor or pot-by-pot into the kitchen sink. Occasionally during those early '40s, Dad would take us to John Ryan's Baths for showers—probably so he could have his bath too—but we did get to swim as well. During the later '40s, we finally moved to a house with a bathtub, but hot water was still used minimally.
Rod Nelson

CHAPTER-SIX CLASS BACKWARDS

Snug as a bug

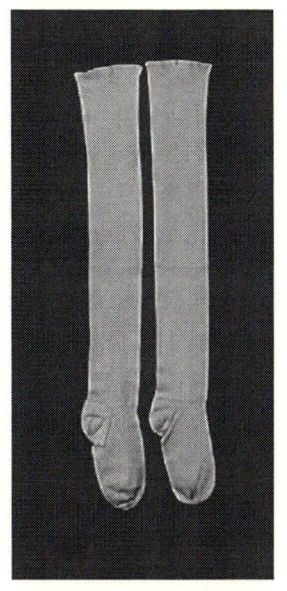

The Church Pair

Toasty Warm—We didn't have central heat in the second floor of the duplex where I lived until I was 12. There was a stove in the kitchen that wood could be burned in on one side for warming the kitchen and we had oil stove in the dining room. In the winters, we shut off our closed-in porch at the front of the house as well as the living room, bringing us closer together for warmth and camaraderie. The bedrooms were cool, so I piled on lots of blankets. I had my own bed, but my two sisters and I all slept in the same room. Every morning during the cold winters, I quickly ran to the kitchen to keep the warmth I gained under the covers during the night. The floors were always frosty on my bare feet, but the kitchen was warm.

Getting dressed for school in the winter was something I vividly remember. I always wore dresses to school. I wore long stockings to keep my legs warm on the walk to and from my elementary school. My mother always had two light brown pairs for everyday wear and one white pair for church. And how did I hold them up? With a convoluted contraption made of white twill cloth straps that went over my shoulders and around my waist! Straps hung down on the front and back of my legs with little metal hooks. These fastened on the stockings so they would stay in place all day. I dressed behind the oil stove where it was nice and warm. My mother would place my clothes on the top of the stove to

(Continued on page 90)

89

(Continued from page 89)

toast them for a bit and I would put them on and be wrapped in snuggly warmth for a time before I had to go outside and walk the three blocks to school.
Carolyn Jodie Hagford

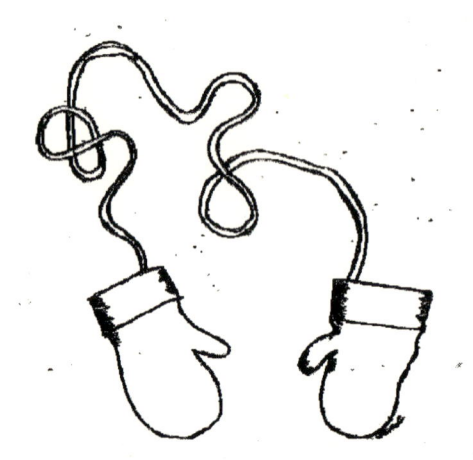

The Things We Wore—My mom bought me corduroy pants to wear to school in the winter. I hated the feel of them on my skin and argued against wearing them. I didn't win. As a little kid, I also had mittens that had a string that ran through the sleeves and behind my neck so that I wouldn't lose them.   **Louie Paff**

Making Do—Making do was darning holes in socks, making rags from old items, crocheting doilies, sewing or mending clothes. This work kept my mother busy until we were taught how to help out with some of it. A sewing machine was ready to go and a basket of mending was always there .
Rod Nelson

Never far away, the mending basket

Gardens

> Because of food shortages from the war, we considered it patriotic to grow our own gardens called, "Victory Gardens." We grew up eating homegrown foods, canning, and sometimes raising our own chickens… delicious food prepared by traditional ways.

Victory Gardens—Of course, there was always the "Victory Garden." to grow your own fruits and vegetables. We had 12 apple trees and a huge garden that my grandmother, Dad, Mom and two brothers worked. Being the only girl, I got to clean up the kitchen, wash, and dry dishes but never had to work in the garden. Thus, my revelation to you, why I never had a green thumb…but does it really matter?
Janet Myrozka Mros

Unidentified men working on their "Victory Garden"

Land Values Families who had come from Europe knew the value of land and how it would help sustain them if treated right. Those people often referred to as DPs (Displaced Persons) used all the land they had to grow food to support their families. To them, lawns were a waste. We had lawns but they were minimal. For all of us, a much better use was planting a garden. Wonderful delicious vegetables came out of the watered seeds and plants.
Carolyn Jodie Hagford

What a Prize—Growing a vegetable garden while trendy now, was a necessity in the '40s. I learned to garden from my aunt and mother. My vegetable garden, with its hand-painted sign made by my dad, was judged a winner in a gardening contest for kids. My photo, taken in the middle of my tomato patch holding a bowl of red tomatoes, was shown at a school assembly. My prize? A bus trip to the Northrup King test gardens in Shakopee where I was given a butternut squash, their latest introduction. **Mary Kranak Cheleen**

Spading Up Old Cans — We helped my mom dig and plant vegetable gardens. When we spaded the soil, we often dug up old rusted cans and broken class bits. Once the garden was leveled and rows were indicated, seeds were planted . As the garden grew the weeding had to be done and often. Carrots, radishes, potatoes, lettuce, beets all supplemented our early diets. Rain water, for watering, was caught in barrels under the gutters or corners of the house.   **Rod Nelson**

Mrs. Nelson at Her Garden

Food-Glorious Food

A Rooster Crows in the Hood—You could raise chickens, as our next-door neighbor did. I awoke to the sound of the rooster crowing early each morning and could hear the clucking of the hens during the day. As you may expect, the neighbors had no lawn, but they always had eggs and o92ccasional chicken dinners .   **Carolyn Jodie Hagford**

Eating Our Pets—Raising chickens was at first fun when we got them as baby chicks at Easter time. But when it came to chasing them for Dad to "do them in," it became very sad. But we had to help mother dip the body into boiling water to begin plucking the feathers.   **Rod Nelson**

Preparing for dinner

Chicken Soup—was one of my grandmother's specialties. I recall helping her scrape the carrots and onions, which were simmered for two days. The chickens were scrubbed and scrubbed under lots of cold water. Then the soup was assembled with water, celery, carrots, and onions and simmered for 2 days. A bowl of grandma's soup was pure heaven. She also made czarnina – duck blood soup. I recall having to hold a large stainless steel bowl to catch the blood while Grandma slit the duck's neck. This was eaten hot on the homemade noodles.   **Bob Peters**

This is as close as you are going to get to seeing the duck's neck slit

Canning—Canning took place every late summer, early fall. The kitchen became busy with tables of whatever vegetables had to be cleaned and cut. Stoves (later put down in the basement) had large pots for heating the vegetables before putting them into jars. Then the jars were put into pressure cookers and sealed with lids. After all the jars were cooled down, they were put on shelves in a dark room in the basement to be brought up during the winter months. Mother was extremely talented in this area. She had the system down and knew how to make my siblings and me part of it. And a greater enjoyment there couldn't be when we ate the various vegetables or fruits later on.   **Rod Nelson**

Tomatoes in the pressure cooker

Shullo's — For some reason our little neighborhood had an abundance of grocery stores. There were at least three stores within two blocks of my house, which was in a total residential area. Delmonico's, Shullo's Leaf Grocery, and Mancino's. Now when I think about it, we didn't have a car part of the time we lived there and probably neither did others. So people shopped at these little stores a lot. **Sue Walker Mandery**

Shullo's Leaf Grocery

Sterzinger's — My parents shopped at a small, independently owned grocery store on 33rd Avenue NE, just east of Central Avenue by a few yards. (There were no giant supermarkets in those days.) I fondly remember the owners Leo and Mabel Sterzinger. Often, when I was of elementary school age, I would have to go to the store for my mother, either on my bike or with the wagon, to get items she needed. Either Leo or Mabel would pick out all the items and bag them. Then all you had to say was "charge it" and be on your way—no plastic credit cards, no cash, or no check was needed. I suppose my parents paid the bill on Friday nights when they got paid. Every once in a while I would be the one to go pay the bill. I remember my mother putting the cash in a mitten and pinning it to my shirt, so I wouldn't lose it on the way. **Bev Warren**

Uncle Arvid's — My dad was a civil engineer and worked for Greyhound. He took the streetcar to work every day. Since we didn't have big grocery stores to shop at, my dad would buy our groceries at Witts (downtown Minneapolis) after work and bring them home on the streetcar. When we ran out of something, we could go to the small corner store owned by Uncle Arvid. One day my mom sent me to the store for "kapusta." Uncle Arvid didn't know what I wanted and I didn't know what else to ask for, so I had to go home and ask my mom what I should get. She told me kapusta was sauerkraut. I had never heard of the word sauerkraut before.

*Witt's downtown market
Courtesy Hennepin County Library,
Special Collections*

Many days my mom would take us over to Columbia Park and we would pick mushrooms. Mom knew which mushrooms were safe to pick and eat. **Nancy Olson Tanner**

The Oak Hill Market — In the '40s, most shopping was done at the corner store – there were lots of them, but they were very small by today's standards – perhaps no larger than a few hundred square feet. They usually had bread and a few other bakery products, a few shelves of canned and packaged products, a cooler (not walk in) with milk and cream etc., a floor model freezer with a door on top for ice cream and Popsicles, a pop cooler and the checkout counter where the candy was. Near our house, the closest corner stores were on 31st, 32nd and 33rd and Johnson. The store on 32nd and Johnson was called Oak Hill. **Dick Myslajek**

Eddie's Corner Store — Between the end of the checkout counter and the ice cream cooler sat another marvel of technology, the soda cooler. Having a number of relatives who were still farming in those days, this device always reminded me of the watering trough for the cows. It was nothing more than a metal tank filled with water and ice and stocked with all varieties of soda. Attached to the front center of this tank was the bottle opener.

All of the soda bottles were sealed with cork lined metal caps. We often snatched some of the discarded bottle caps, pulled the cork lining out of the cap, and then pressed the cap onto our T-shirts, using the cork liner from behind the shirt to secure the cap. All afternoon the entire gang would be festooned with bottle cap "buttons."

A candy case sat on the checkout counter. This was a two-shelved glass case with a sloping front and doors in the rear. In order to get your candy you would have to tell Eddie that you wanted one cent worth of this or two cents worth of that. But the "this" and "that" were wondrous delicacies.

Front and center in the candy case where the licorice whips. These were approximately six-inch long pieces of twisted licorice candy. They came in either red or black though at the moment I can't recall any difference in their flavor. I do remember taking the beginnings of a bite and just letting your teeth hold the candy

(Continued on page 98)

(Continued from page 97)

while you pulled on it and stretched it out. I can't remember for the life of me why we did that. Maybe it was in the mistaken idea that we got more candy that way. You will remember, of course, Tootsie Rolls —candy I still have difficulty passing up— and the Tootsie Roll Pops, a bit of Tootsie Roll that was stuck on a stick and coated with a layer of candy. Did you ever manage not to bite into it ? Coke bottles were small wax models filled with the syrup. You accessed the syrup by biting the head off the bottle.

Once you had slurped up the syrup, you would chew the wax to extract the last scintilla of flavor. Then there were the Mary Jane's, those bite-sized peanut butter and molasses candies wrapped in a red and yellow paper with a picture of Mary Jane on it. And, of course, there were individual pieces of Bazooka bubble gum. Bazooka was always the best of all the available bubble gum. Not only did it blow great bubbles but you also got a small cartoon with it. Two pieces of Bazooka and your jaws would ache for hours but not as bad as the giant jaw-breakers, those huge balls of sweet that would break your teeth if you actually tried to break the outside with your teeth.

Rounding out the candy case's collection were the wax lips and a set of sugar extrusions affixed to a paper carrier that we called candy buttons. Of course, the sidewalk

(Continued on page 99)

(Continued from page 98)

outside the store would end up with dirty lumps of chewed wax.

Yes, I was guilty of spitting my wax on the sidewalk. I learned how to do it by watching some of the older kids in the neighborhood. Maybe we all learn some dirty habits because older kids were doing it. I automatically assumed it was a cool thing to do. You could tell Eddie to give you one, two, or three cents worth of candy buttons, and he would unroll the appropriate length of paper and tear it off. We then ambled down the street talking to one another about the important issues of the day and, one by one, nibbling the candy buttons from the paper. I expect that this paper may well have ended up in some of the blowing trash that someone had to pick up

Parents were concerned that playing with the pretend cigarettes would lead to a nasty addiction later on. I am not certain whether it was the pretend cigarettes or the fact that my favorite uncle — the epitome of all cool dudes — was a smoker that led to my addiction. But my prepubescent self never considered any of that. I was just enthralled with what my pennies and nickels could procure for me at Eddie's Corner Store. **Larry Kohout**

Rolig's Drug Store — Pop was nonexistent for us in the late '40s, early '50s, except on Saturday night when I was sent to the corner Rolig's drugstore on 13th Avenue and 4th Street about 7:00 at night to pick up the early Minneapolis Sunday Tribune and a six-pack of bottled Barqs Creme Soda. (I called it Barges since that is what my mom called it.) Always creme soda—one bottle for each member of the family. **Rod Nelson**

Blackey's Bakery — Many immigrants settled in this area Minneapolis. They were Polish, Russian, and Slovaks. Also, many were from Sweden and Norway. There was a wonderful little store on the corner 24th Avenue and Monroe. I spent most of my money I received returning *empty* pop bottles for candy. Blackey's Bakery was not far from our house. My mom sent me there often. They opened at 3:00 p.m. so after school I would get warm rye bread that we just loved. Everything was within walking distance from our house. There was a library, a theater, the cleaners, a bank, and many different kinds of shopping. It was a very convenient neighborhood. **Nadia Lewacko Yantos**

13th Avenue Bakery — Perhaps the real treat of the week during the same period was fresh bakery goods. That consisted of one loaf of white bread not sliced, a loaf of rye sliced, and a dozen fresh rolls. Being the one sent to the 13th Avenue bakery mid Saturday mornings, I got to pick out the rolls. Well almost; we needed long-johns and Bismarck's — which for us were pretty standard, although some jelly-filled figure eights would be requested. **Rod Nelson**

Bridgeman's — Ah, yes, Bridgeman's—the source of delicious ice cream goodies in our youth. I remember going many, many times for their 25¢ chocolate malts made with vanilla ice cream. When I could afford it on a hot summer day, I'd go for the marble sundae. They were more expensive than a malt, and I'm thinking they were 45¢, though it may have been 35¢. **Louie Paff**

Ready Meats
AN OLD FASHION MEAT MARKET

Morin's — Whenever we needed groceries, I would cut through the neighborhood alleys and walk two blocks to Morin's store. They all knew my family and would welcome me coming in so I could read them my mom's list. No one could figure out her writing but me! We bought special cuts of meat from Ready's Meat Market on Johnson Street. **Carol Lyons Larson**

National Tea — It wasn't until I was about 9 that I can remember shopping days. By then we had moved to Broadway and 4th Street. There would be those days Dad and Mom got in the car and when they came back, she would come up to the backdoor and tell us to "Go help your Dad take the bags of groceries in." Actually, there were bags and bags to feed a family of six. So even though I don't recall them shopping before then, we must have eaten.

There were those Saturdays when my sister, brother, and I got to ride with Mom and Dad to National Tea on University Avenue just off East Hennepin. I really don't recall seeing so many cars in a parking lot just sitting there before then. Mom would go in while Dad catnapped in the car. We looked out the window at people and cars. It seemed like years later that she would come out and Dad would help load the bags into the car. I eagerly awaited those Saturdays when I could say "I don't want to go" and got to stay home. But if I was around when they came home, I still had to help unload the car.

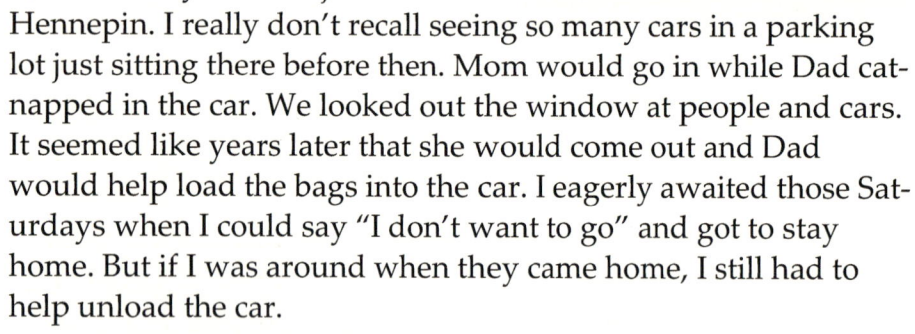

The food got put away on shelves in the cupboards and in the refrigerator. Of course, there was always the fight amongst us kids as to who would get to burst the orange bubble in the Oleomargarine and knead the plastic bag into butter. It felt good to know that there would be times I could sneak some spoonfuls of sugar or steal a cookie—though hard to reach—from the Howdy Doody cookie jar on top of the refrigerator. **Rod Nelson**

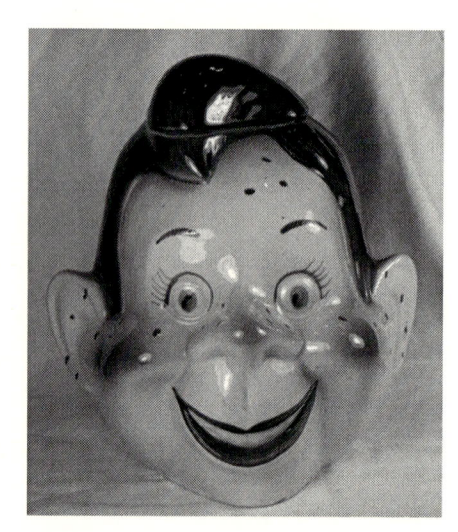

The Mall or Not — The first super market to open was near 29th and Johnson —a National Tea—which would probably fit into the produce section of today's super markets. I remember shopping with my mother carrying large sacks of groceries the half-mile to our house. Your arms felt like they would fall off. The closest thing we had to a mall was on 29th and Johnson where there was a drugstore, five and dime, hardware store, cleaners, barber shop, plumbing shop, hamburger joint, gas station, bakery, dentist, insurance broker. When we got bicycles, we would bike to the drugstore for a milk shake or malt – 25 cents or 30 cents (large). You got a large glass full and extra on the side in the malt can. Ice cream cones cost five or ten cents. The hamburger place was attached to the Pure Oil station – hamburger steak or hot turkey plate about a buck. Franks haircut cost a buck. **Dick Myslajek**

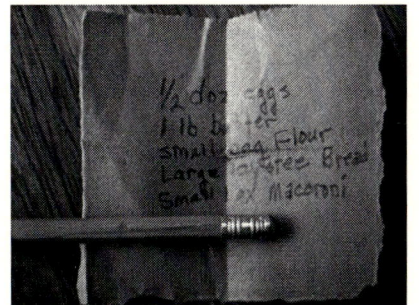

What's a Credit Card — It was around 1948-49. There was a small grocery store with an old fashioned butcher shop inside. It was located on Brighton Avenue, around 27th, about 2 ½ blocks south of St. Anthony Blvd. We (my sister and/or I alone) were sent with a note from Mom to give to the butcher. Sometimes there were a few extra groceries on the list. Dad was paid only once monthly and Mom was able to charge the groceries here. I had no clue as to the hard times at home. I distinctly remember the atmosphere was very friendly and I always felt okay to hand my note to the butcher and receive my groceries. **Kathleen Coveney Fields**

Shopping? — I don't remember. I don't think we did that. **Norm Solberg**

Home Deliveries

Without freezers, it was almost a necessity to have ice and dairy products delivered to our houses by trucks. One of the perks of our childhood.

The Iceman Cometh — Until I was 10, we used an ice box instead of a refrigerator. Ours was a white device with a Formica type material covering the outside (more expensive ones were made of oak) shaped like a refrigerator, but instead of having a compressor and refrigerant it had a large compartment in the top to hold blocks of ice. The compartment was on the top because cold air is heavier than warm air and therefore it falls, keeping the food below relatively cold. Simple but ingenious. You may think we didn't have any ice cubes for beverages in those days, and you would be right. But we used an ice pick to break off small pieces of ice to cool our beverages in hot weather or when my parents wanted to have a mixed drink.

The ice box worked quite well, and I don't remember ever throwing out food for its having gone bad by being too warm. Need leads to creative inventions, and the ice box was a good solution to

(Continued on page 105)

(Continued from page 104)

the need to keep food cold. Ice cream was purchased and consumed at the local Dairy Queen.

How did we get our ice? An ice man came every other day on his old horse-drawn wagon with many blocks of ice on it. I loved to see him come when I was small because it was an opportunity to see a horse. I was intrigued by that. The ice man had a good idea of how much space the ice compartment in each customer's ice box had, and would select blocks that he thought would fit. He'd use his ice tongs, an oversized pliers-type of tool with the handles being rounded so one could get ones hands into the rounded part. With the tongs, he'd pick up a block of ice, sling it over his back, and haul it up the steps to our second floor apartment. If we still had a fair amount of ice left the ice man would chip at it with an ice pick and break it into small pieces that could fit around the block he had brought. A pan in the bottom of the ice box had a drain to the bottom where a bucket would collect the water from the melted ice.

Where did ice come from in those days? It came from lakes, cut out in the winter, and stored in buildings where ice was covered with sawdust. It was a good method, and ice from the winter lasted throughout the summer, providing many homes with ice for their ice boxes. **Louie Paff**

Ice (Mis) Appropriation — Stealing ice from back of truck or wagon was a skill indeed. Timing of the driver delivering to the house and returning was crucial to a successful grabbing of ice chunks within reach. However there were times when one had to jump into the truck and grab a pick and chip away but quickly. I can't remember if we ever got caught. **Larry Kohout**

Ice Thief

Skimming the Cream — The milkman delivered our milk in a truck. We loved skimming the cream off the top of the glass bottles. On hot days, I remember the iceman bringing us chunks of ice and carrying it down to our icebox in the basement.
Carol Lyons Larson

Milk in Gallon Jugs — Our family had home milk delivery when I was very young. I remember when the dairy replaced the round, tapered neck bottles with squarish one quart bottles. It was delivered to the back door, from the alley, and our refrigerator (vintage General Electric of about 1937) was handy on the back landing. The refrigerator replaced an icebox about the time my parents and sister moved there in 1937. When I was about 9 or so, a dairy store opened on Stinson Boulevard and 19th and we began getting milk in gallon jugs there at a considerably reduced price. **Bob Buntrock**

You Put a Sign in the Window — Some of you probably could afford a real refrigerator but we couldn't. We had an ice box. The ice man would come around certain days of the week and if you needed ice, you put a sign in the window and he would deliver to you the exact amount you needed. When refrigerators came into being we still could not afford one, so went with the ice-man! **Carolyn Jodie Hagford**

Mealtimes

> Someone once said, we didn't have "fast food." it was all slow. But so was life and so we had time with our families.

Slow Food Together — I have many favorite memories of growing up, but one special one was mealtime. Obviously, the good food my mom prepared was a favorite, as she was an excellent cook, but the time spent at the table was the special time. It was a time to discuss the day for all of us. We talked about school, homework, and my friends. Of course, being an only child gave me The Spotlight. My parents were always interested in what I had to say, which was great for me. That was one advantage of being an only child. My dad and mom also spoke about their day and this made for great family unity. **Jean Torgerson Strong**

After Supper — My memories of evenings were sitting around the living room after supper after the dishes were done, listening to the radio (we didn't get a TV until I was 13). Dad would be reading the paper, Mom would be doing handwork, and my sister and I would be drawing. Marlene (Edison '49) was a good artist and even though I wasn't, she'd encourage me to draw, usually with crayons on a tablet. I owe my love of color, pattern, and appreciation of art in general to her. **Bob Buntrock**

Meals Were Special — The first things that come to mind are meals together –it was a priority—especially dinner every evening and Saturday breakfast. We always sat down together for the whole meal. And, for many years, we had a picnic table in the back yard. In the summer, my father would grill and we would eat outside often enjoying summer food like potato salad, iced tea, and fresh vegetables. **Dick Myslajek**

Chores

Fed and well fed, we found lots of ways of staying busy or entertaining ourselves in our homes and yards. We also had plenty of chores to do around the house. There were no dryers or automatic washing machines in those days, no dishwashers. If we ever said we were bored, they would put us to work! Some of us in The Valley would get picked up in a truck to work on farms.

Crank a Wringer — By the time I was in sixth grade, my mom was teaching me how to crank carefully a wringer washer and how to pluck feathers off turkeys by hand for Thanksgiving dinner. In our daily life, we had neither TV nor computers for distraction. What we did have was plenty of time to talk to each other. My days with my mom were well spent hearing about the people we knew. I learned from her the art of studying character and listening to her stories. **Carol Lyons Larson**

Basement Clotheslines — Our four-plex building's basement had a laundry room with four of those old cement/zinc sinks facing together in pairs in the middle, and each tenant's washing machine was against a wall when not being used. A long room off the laundry room had clotheslines for drying clothes in the winter. When small, the neighbor girl and I would attach our roller skates to our shoes and we'd have fun roller-skating in that drying room. **Louie Paff**

Burning Leaves — Burning barrels were part of everyone's backyard. We burned everything, even though there were some restrictions. Not sure what? Leaf burning in the fall was done by everyone everywhere. Fires were seen in the alleys, street gutters, and backyards. What fun, what wonderful smells. What ? danger? **Rod Nelson**

Celebrating fall — I suppose to some, raking and burning leaves in the fall would be considered a chore. But if I were asked to organize an event to celebrate the season, I would go collect a pile of fallen leaves and burn it. Almost everyone burned their leaves, often off the curb to the street and no one complained that I know of. To me, nothing brings back pleasant memories of the fall more than the waft of burning leaves. **Dick Myslajek**

You Gotta Take a Break — As children, we knew the value of money. My parents would pay us to do chores around the house. I think I got a dollar for mowing the lawn. I remember how it seemed like a huge chore to me, so I'd make myself a pitcher of lemonade, go once around the yard with my push mower, stop for lemonade, and go on. It took a long time to mow the lawn that way, but made it more fun. **Norm Solberg**

In summer — My chores included watering the tree, mowing the lawn with a push mower, and going to the corner store often for milk, bread, or a can of something, for which I got to buy myself something for a nickel, like a Popsicle or bottle of pop (only 7 ounces then.)

Every yard had posts with multiple clothes-lines used to dry clothes summer and winter. The clothes were washed often on Mondays with a hand cranked wringer washer.

Many housewives ironed sheets, towels, and hankies. I think my mom gave up on that since she worked full time. **Dick Myslajek**

7 Ounce Coke Bottle

CHAPTER-SIX　　　　　　　　　　　　　　　　　　　　CLASS BACKWARDS

Hickey's — When I was about 7 and living on 2nd Street and 15th Avenue, I would be sent on a short trip for some food from Hickey's corner store only a block and half away. Mom had prepared a list on a piece of scratch paper she had creased and torn from a larger piece of scratch paper, sometimes from paper bags. I held this piece of folded paper tightly in my little hand as I went on my way. The list was short and the total size and weight was possible for me to carry back. Maybe it was based on what Mom could afford from the food allowance Dad had given her for that week. Hickey's had one of those grabbing poles now used quite efficiently by the elderly to reach items on the high shelves, usually boxes. Once placed on the counter, each item was written down in their tablet for our family and kept in a small wooden file box. He flipped it open page by page, 'til a new sheet was exposed. I loved the sound of those pages flipping and the box being hit by the tablet. Those monthly bills must have been paid for by someone very generous in the neighborhood, for I can't remember my parents going to Hickey's to pay the bill. It was his store that introduced me to Popsicle Pete—bag, sticks, and all, which we collected from the gutters. We made things from the sticks and sent the bags in for prizes. **Rod Nelson**

111

From Radishes to Riches — During the summertime, the kids in our neighborhood were picked up by a truck, and given a ride to various farms in the Twin City area where we picked radishes, put a rubber binder around them, and later put them into a bushel, earning 25 cents per bushel. 108 bunches equaled a bushel. Later, we were put on a truck to return to Kristoff's farm. There we would grab four bunches of radishes floating in huge tanks of water, sometimes three feet deep. We'd shake the water out, and put 100 bunches back into a bushel basket, ready for market.
David Larson

CHAPTER SEVEN:
CAN JOHNNY COME OUT AND PLAY?

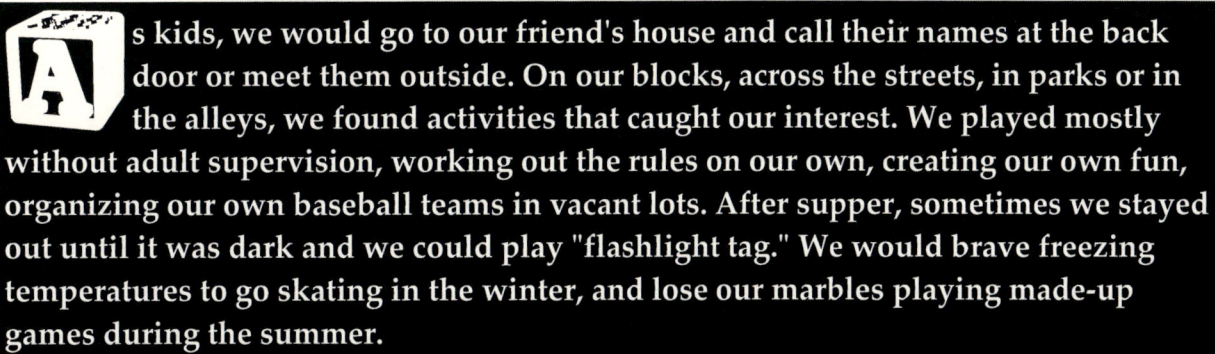

As kids, we would go to our friend's house and call their names at the back door or meet them outside. On our blocks, across the streets, in parks or in the alleys, we found activities that caught our interest. We played mostly without adult supervision, working out the rules on our own, creating our own fun, organizing our own baseball teams in vacant lots. After supper, sometimes we stayed out until it was dark and we could play "flashlight tag." We would brave freezing temperatures to go skating in the winter, and lose our marbles playing made-up games during the summer.

Neighborhood houses became our hangouts. Camp Fire girls and Scout troops provided fun and camaraderie. In our homes, we played board games together, and when we didn't have anything else to do, we used our imagination to create the kind of fun we would remember our whole life long.

Games We Played On Our Own

Oh! The Good Old Days! — What I remember about growing up in the '40s and '50s was that we all felt so safe in our neighborhoods. For one thing we didn't have to lock our doors—ever. We didn't lock our car doors either. We knew who our neighbors were, and they were like our own family. We walked in and out of each others' houses without knocking on their door. All of us kids could play outside at night in the dark and not be afraid of anyone harming us. And a quarter could get us into the movie theater and even have money left over to buy popcorn.   **Ann Shleisman Booth**

Creative Fun — For each season we had outdoor games and we had indoor games. Most of them were made-up games…games for which we made up our own rules. Some, of course, like Monopoly, had rules. All of our games and play, however, had an element of imagination.

There you are… games and play! Season to season, indoors to outdoors. All of them required creativity and friends. I'm sure that each little neighborhood or group of friends had their own little games and rules. All of them kept our minds active and our growing bodies healthy. In the winter, we went skating at Logan Park and St. Anthony rinks by my house, and

(Continued on page 115)

(Continued from page 114)

tobogganing at Columbia Golf Course. I still have my toboggan. We went to the Saturday and Sunday matinees at the Ritz Theater, which by the way only cost only 12¢ and 25¢. We had wiener roasts and picnics and Friday night dances at Sheridan School. We went swimming at John Ryan's pool and roller skating at indoor rinks or outside.
Sharron Matt Weglinski

Lotsa Fun — If we talk about outside games, they were not with family members as much as neighborhood kids, although sometimes Dad would actually take us over to Sheridan field and hit balls for us to catch. Neighbors' yards were off limits. I was afraid to cut through one. I don't think I even knew any adult neighbors that I would stop to talk with.

Games like Kick the Can were played in the alleys with garage walls, fences, large trees, and bushes serving as some of the hiding places. You remained "it" until you had spotted everyone. Once spotted, you sat and waited for the rest to be caught. But if not caught sneaked up and kicked the can, all were free to go hide again. You were still "it."   **Rod Nelson**

The Best of Times — The summers of my childhood were the best of times interrupted only by nine months of school. Nothing was ever organized— it was pure spontaneity. After breakfast and getting dressed, you would go outside and if no

(Continued on page 116)

(Continued from page 115)
one was there, you would go to someone's house and call their name from outside. When we were younger, it would be wagons or tricycles or roller skates or cowboys and Indians or war or Hide and Seek or running around in all the empty lots in the neighborhood ad infinitum. When we were a little older, if there were enough of a quorum, then it would be touch football or baseball (bounce-out or two or three man scrub in the street) interrupted by the occasional heads-up for a car. The street was our playground. At night, we played games like Sixty or Run Sheep Run or games we made up and didn't have a name. On hot days, board games or card games were played under a shady tree. We knew how to find the Big Dipper and the North Star and the Little Dipper and saw our shadow from the moon. And then school started again.
Dick Myslajek

Annie — Annie Over — I didn't realize how special it was to be able to play outside, in yards, on sidewalks and side streets, and in parks and vacant lots. Another childhood game was Annie Annie Over. Two players stood on opposite sides of a building (garage or low house) and threw the ball over the roof, hopefully without touching the roof, announced by yelling "Annie Annie Over." Red Light, Green Light also involved instructions. Players could move forward when someone called, "Green Light" but had to stop on "Red Light." I only remember playing this on a long flight of stairs. Of course, there was always Tag or Hide and Seek, both being more fun as it became dark. **Bob Buntrock**

Places to Play

A Playground Called Yardville — During the summer years, 1948 through 1951, the Margaret Barry House in Northeast Minneapolis tried a new type of playground for the neighborhood kids in the Edith Cavell Grade School district. The park was located on the 3400 block, between Fillmore and Pierce Streets, just north of the school. I'm not sure what the official name of the park was, but we called it "Yardville." The object of the park was to allow the kids to stake out a land claim and build something on it. The Margaret Barry House provided an adult supervisor and mentor (Don Hamergren) and local businesses donated materials such as lumber, tools, nails and other items needed to build a house (shack). While this sounds like a purely male-focused activity, you would be surprised how many girls participated. During that first summer, many shacks were in progress and some were quite elaborate. The first two summers were very successful and a lot of attention was given by the local and national media. Kids got on local television, like the Arlie Haberle talk show and PBS. National magazines like Look and Life covered the project, and some of the kids got their pictures published working on their creations. Even President Truman toured the project when he was in town. However, after the first two summers, the project started to deteriorate. Material donations were in short supply. Vandalism started after the first

Carolyn Bak and Ralph Fuerst start nailing the siding on their shack.

As shown in the October 1950 McCall's magazine

(Continued on page 118)

(Continued from page 117)

year and a fence had to be put up. The Yardville Bureau of Investigation (YBI) was started by the kids in the program who took turns watching the park for vandals and reported them to Don. After Edith Cavell School closed permanently, participation dropped off enough to close the Park. It was a grand experiment while it lasted.
Dale Halverson (Class of '56)

Yardville – AKA The Yard — By the time I first saw the ground around the Edith Cavell School, the school had burned down and all traces of Yardville were gone. My only knowledge of Yardville came from an article published in a 1950 edition of *McCall's Magazine* my mother had shown me. While a number of my friends talked about Yardville, the magazine article called the place "The Yard." McCall's sponsored the project with a $15,000 donation and the "Bug House" (the Margaret Barry House) provided the adult supervision. Local businesses donated scrap building material and Yardville was born.

That supervision dealt with passing out tools and materials, and assigning building plats to the youngsters. From that point on the kids were on their own to build whatever they wanted to build. According to the article, after an initial period of competition and stealing of materials between shacks, kids learned that cooperation worked better

Harry Forsythe lays first sill before partner John Kraft finishes tough job of excavating in hard clay.
As shown in the October 1950 McCall's magazine

(Continued on page 119)

Chapter Seven — Class Backwards

Girls proved such good builders that early anti-feminist movement died out. Patty Kellerman, Patty Iverson and Diane Koelfgen start a house.

As shown in the October 1950 McCall's magazine

Jimmy Barry finds he is up to using a man-size saw. He is one of more than 200 children that used the playground.

As shown in the October 1950 McCall's magazine

(Continued from page 118)

than competition and most of the raiding of materials came to an end

One of the things provided by the magazine and the adult supervision was a fence that surrounded the property to keep night raiding to a minimum. However, the friends I talked with about this said that the fence did little to stop the raiding; mostly the raiding was controlled by the kids themselves.

The whole idea for The Yard originated in Denmark where a couple of teachers decided that kids in the city needed a place to be creative. As the Second World War ended they developed a project that gave kids a piece of empty ground and some scrap building material, then let them do whatever they wanted to do with those materials. The editors at McCall's weren't sure that this idea would work in the US. They finally set up a demonstration project and chose Nordeast Minneapolis to do the demonstration. They obviously recognized the innate creativity of Nordeast kids.

Larry Kohout

Streets — Cleveland Street in front of my house was the site for many softball and football games. There didn't seem to be much traffic, and we'd just move to the side when a car came along. Sometimes we'd go to the playground and have a little more space. I was never a jock, but I had a lot of fun playing. I remember Gary Peterson, who was a jock, helping me out. He'd lift his front foot just like Kirby Puckett later did, before he smashed a home run. Ron Willow and John Ostenso lived just two blocks away, and Mike and Eddie Solz were a few houses down, so they were often there for the games. I remember Mike and Ron almost got into a fight once, and I had to remind them that we were all friends and neighbors. **Norm Solberg**

Norm's street of mediation. Norm's house is on the left.

*Curb and gutter laid through cow pasture as city expands north and east.
courtesy of the Minnesota Historical Society*

The Edge of a City — We lived at 29th and McKinley Street. One block East was Stinson Blvd. and literally, it was the end of the city. There were fields and farms to the east. We used to play ball on a triangle of land on 30th Stinson Blvd. I thought it was a huge piece of land...well it was, to a 10-year-old. I don't remember teams or even scores in the games, just waiting for my turn to bat and hoping I could hit it a long way. Two or three of us would walk north about one mile following Stinson Blvd. to the Salvation Army Camp. If we went in the spring, before any activity there, we could play by Silver Lake, catch snakes and frogs and look in the cabins. It was very exciting,

(Continued on page 121)

(Continued from page 120)

especially if we did not get caught. When the building did come in the early '50s, we would explore the new houses being built. It was so fun to walk through the rooms especially when just the studs were put up. This was strictly a not-allowed activity both by parents and the builders. We did get caught and warned to stay away, but it was so much fun! **Kathleen Coveney Fields**

Current photo of Kathleen Coveney Fields' home. The porch didn't exist in her times in the house.

Golf Courses — My friends Roger Johnson and John Ostenso and I were big game hunters, trapping muskrats at the swamp out on Highway 8 in New Brighton and gophers at the Gross Golf Course. A typical day during the summer would have us riding our bikes to the swamp, setting the muskrat traps, and proceeding on with our gopher hunting equipment and golf club sets to Gross Golf Course. Gross had a practice hole and, as we did not have enough money to play the regular course, we would play nine holes on the practice hole. Then, after the ranger kicked us off of the practice hole, we proceeded home to let the gophers and muskrats free. This is the only reason I can think of that we became Gopher sports fans! **Ron Willow**

Alleys — We used the alleys and backyards to play Tag, Hide and Go Seek, or Kick the Can until it got dark most summer nights. We felt safe and secure—everyone knew every family. No one got in much trouble—well except for some Halloween tricks I'd rather not talk about. **Bob Peters**

Scary Spots — I have such a fondness for the memories of alleys in my youth. If you were lucky enough to have an alley, that was generally the way you entered your home-- of course that is where the garages were. The alley was also the fast way in and out of a property where there might be an apple tree. And in the dark of night, if you had to walk by the alley it could be a scary spot. Mom always said to go to the middle of the street if you were afraid. But I think it is sad they don't put in alleys anymore. **Kathleen Coveney Fields**

More Alleys — Lot fronts 44-foot throughout our neighborhood, there was no room for driveways on the sides of houses so alleys were a necessity. The alleys in our neighborhood were a place to play even in the winter. Besides our action games, we'd play baseball in the alleys. Later, we'd play catch with either baseballs or footballs. Dad had a garage built when I was 10 and put up a basketball backboard. Since our driveway was crushed limestone, the only pavement around was the alley so dribbling to the basket was almost impossible.

During a late winter thaw, the double tire track ruts in the alleys carried daytime creeks. We'd come home from school and break out the toy boats and float them down the steam. Our T-shaped alley was particularly well suited to this pastime since the slope was gently down the stem of the T and then turned left past our driveway. In addition to the icy base of these canyons, there was always some slush available so we'd channel and dam the stream, even put in locks to prolong the down slope ride of the boats. Some of the kids from other neighborhoods without such convenient streams were handy with woodwork and custom-designed boats for sailing. Curious that our neighborhood didn't produce more hydraulic engineers. **Bob Buntrock**

Winter Sports

Speeders And Figure Skaters — When winter came, our tennis courts and playing fields were flooded creating three large ice rinks. One was enclosed with the hockey boards for hockey only. Of course, sometimes we did sneak on it even though we did not have hockey skates on.

We sometimes went skating right after school, but more often because we were young teenagers we went at night. Temperature did not really matter. But the kind of skates did. If you played hockey, you wore hockey skates; otherwise, the girls wore figure skates and the boys wore speeders. They were influenced by the Silver Skaters' Minneapolis competition that Ken Bartholomew was famous for. It didn't matter for me. I couldn't keep my ankles off the ice with either, but I wore those speeders to be like the other boys.

Not only were my ankles not skaters' ankles, but my ability to stop was less than perfect, which made me appreciate the snowbanks piled high around the rink. Executing turns slowly did work though, and even produced a gradual stop. But in spite of no training and not realizing you could be taught these things, the whole evening was fun. Logan was the only rink we really went to. Not sure if we aware of

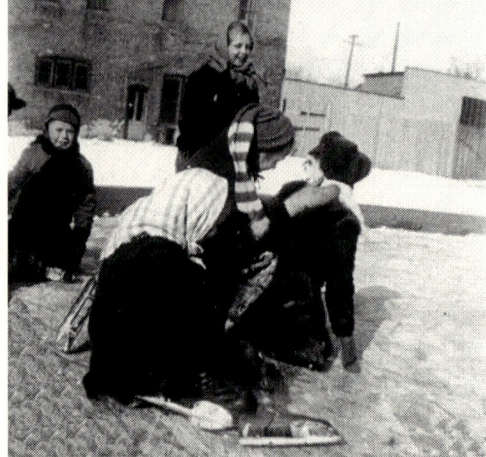

(Continued on page 125)

(Continued from page 124)

anywhere else to skate or even if there were others besides Powderhorn.

Tag, chasing, stealing hats or scarves of anyone, crack the whip all kept us busy. No skating by couples, although some of that was going on over at the other rink.
Rod Nelson

Slush And Runny Noses — Our indoor and outdoor games and playtime activities were dictated by the season. There was no such thing as daylight saving time or wind chills. When it got dark, we came in from outside. When it got cold, our scarves got icy stiff from our runny noses and breath.

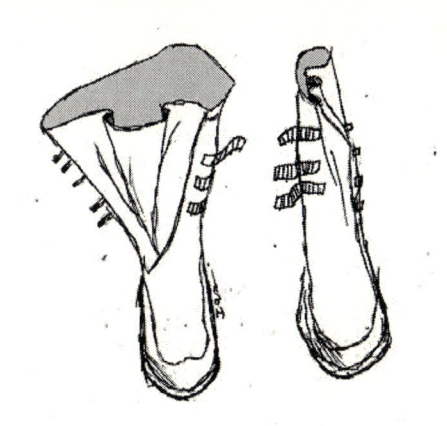

Shortly after Christmas, we dug out last year's ice skates or talked our parents into going to the Skate Exchange for new skates, or should I say "new" used skates. We rubbed the blades with sandpaper to make them sharper, tied them together with their laces, hung them around our neck and walked over to the park in our black rubber boots with the clanky snap buckles. We sat on outdoor benches and changed into our skates and ankled around our sheet of bumpy ice.

(Continued on page 126)

Bumpy Ice Rink—How dumb were we?

(Continued from page 125)

Note: it was bumpy because soon after the Park Board people flooded the football field to make an ice skating rink, and just as it began to freeze, some of us thought it was fun to throw snowballs into the half frozen water. This, of course, produced a slurping splash in the half frozen field. We laughed and laughed and had a great time. However, it froze that way. It froze and it stayed bumpy and rough all winter long…how dumb were we? **Bob Peters**

Warming Houses — The basement of Logan was turned into a warming house with a stove and wooden floor. The warm, humid, musty smell of the room added to the continual pounding of skates on the floor. On the wooden benches all around, we helped each other put on our skates. Remember? Holding your thumb or fingers against the laces allowed your friend to lace them up tight.

Actually, we were much more willing to help the girls with theirs. Leather choppers were in but not for the girls. They had to deal with soggy knitted mittens or gloves. At the end of the evening our groups would split up to walk home back down 13th Avenue or Broadway or Monroe or Adams with our skates' laces tied together and our skates hung around our neck. **Rod Nelson**

The Hollows — I can't believe our parents let us walk in the dark if we decided to go skating after supper. It would've been unthinkable for us to ask them to give us a ride. We never heard of "windchill." If we decided to go skating, and were willing to walk half a mile to get there, I guess they figured it couldn't be that cold.

Our skating rinks were in the center of two hollows at the bottom of a hill by Thomas Lowry Grade School. Between the two of them, a temporary wooden warming house had been erected. As we entered, hisses of steam emitted from the wood burning stove. Wet smelly socks with a funky odor were drying on a pole in front of it. Raucous voices from other kids our age were clashing with the sound of their skates stomping on the wooden floor, as they went in and out the door. We would find a place to sit down to remove our shoes and step into our skates. Once outside, the lights seemed to have visible halos surrounding them, and distant voices echoed across the ice. It was magic. It was magic, especially skating with someone you liked a lot . **Carol Lyons Larson**

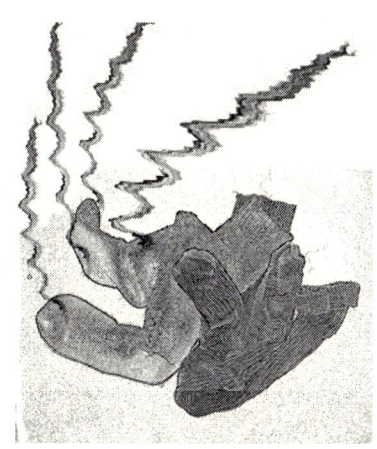

Skating To Music — In the winter we went skating at Logan Park. They played wonderful music and it could be heard while we skated. Also, in back of my house, I built four individual rooms of snow and my sled was used for a bed. The yard had perfect boundaries—a hedge was on two sides and a walkway on the other two. It was an area that was protected from the wind as well.
Jean Torgerson Strong

Crack The Whip — As we got older, Logan Park became the place for ice skating in the winter. The big softball field was flooded and made an excellent recreational skating rink. Crack the Whip was a favorite game when we had enough people. It was always scary being on the end, so I opted to be in the middle of the line. We spent many hours skating there both during the daytime and after dark. **Louie Paff**

Sleigh Ride in Columbia Park
Image courtesy of the Minnesota Historical Society

Death Valley — In the winter I remember walking down to Columbia Park after dark with the other kids to toboggan down the icy hill we called, "Death Valley." I'll never forget getting my hand caught in a rope and being dragged down to the bottom of the hill in the dark of night. Other nights we walked to Audubon Park to skate. I was not an accomplished skater, but at the skating rink you could retreat to the warming house to warm up. I bet the smell of the wood fire in the stove and leather choppers drying from that heat will stay with us all forever. One of the experiences I vividly remember was attending a birthday party sleigh ride one night. The team of horses and sleigh arrived at our friends' houses and drove us around on snowy city streets. You needed to make sure you were not close to the edge of the sleigh.
Dodd Knutsen (Class of '59)

CHAPTER - SEVEN CLASS BACKWARDS

Camp Fire Girls and Snow — Claire Hudoba's mother was our wonderful Camp Fire Girls leader. She was amazing. We would take our cardboard from an old box and go to the Columbia Golf Course and slide down the hill for hours. What fun.

Another activity was selling the delicious Camp Fire Girl donuts. Micki Havrish and I would go from house to house selling them. We got the giggles so badly that we couldn't even say anything, and those sweet people would buy them anyway! As a kid, I just took for granted the wonderful experiences she provided. As an adult, I wish I could tell her thank you.

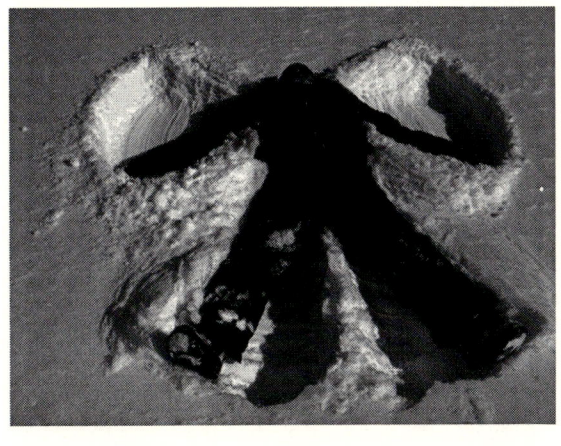

It seems many of my memories involve the Minnesota snow that I actually now miss. I so remember the wonderful walks in the snow. As soon as the snow would begin to fall, either Micki Havrish (now Foster) would call me or I would call her and we would walk miles in the snow, stop to make angels in the snow, taste a few flakes, and generally just appreciate the beauty. The '40s were great times, weren't they? We tried to avoid the snowballs thrown at us by those "mean boys" we liked a lot. Elaine Theisen and I often built snow forts in her backyard and stocked them with snowballs. Does anyone ever remember getting cold as a child? I don't.
Mary Ann Tema Weinberger

Summer sports

The Soap Box Derby — Growing up on University Avenue N.E. during the 1940s, it was always a treat when Dad took our Larson family for a ride on St. Anthony Blvd., now known as St. Anthony Pkwy. At Central Avenue, the road wound up the hill to Fillmore Street. At Pierce Street we always screeched as the car went down the Big Hill to Buchanan and then turned a few short blocks to the drugstore at 29th and Johnson Street where ice cream cones were three scoops for a nickel.

The Big Hill was where the Soap Box Derby was held each summer. Boys built racing cars out of orange crates and miscellaneous wood. I think the wheels were from old wagons. I never knew that soap boxes were made of wood, but that is how the Soap Box Derby got its name.

On the appointed Saturday boys participated in elimination heats until finally someone was chosen to advance to the national competition in Akron, Ohio. My brothers and I never made a soap box, but our cousin, Junior Semanko, did. He was about 10 years older than I was, and he was sort of an older brother because our mother took care of him and his three older sisters after their mother died when Junior was a baby.

The race started on Pierce Street at the top of the steep hill

Saint Anthony Boulevard looking west

And it begins

(Continued on page 131)

Three unidentified drivers in their mighty machines

(Continued from page 130)

that ends at the next block, Buchanan Street. As I recall, the finish line was beyond Buchanan – I think at the next block, which is Lincoln. A few even made it to the next street, Johnson, which was a busy thoroughfare. All through the area streets were cordoned off to keep automobiles and other vehicles away from the race area.

When our family moved to a newly built residence in the summer of 1950, it was ironical that it was on Buchanan Street, half a block north of the Big Hill that we Larson boys so loved.   **Norman Larson (Class of '52)**

Wildlife — When the weather warmed up, in addition to the wetlands, open fields where Waite Park is now located were inhabited with meadowlarks and other wildlife. We used to play all around the area with its mixture of woods, wetlands, and fields, going to Silver Lake or as far away as Lake Johanna. We would fish from the shore or watch men fishing from the shore catching sunfish or bullheads. It was always a challenge taking the bullhead off the hook.
Dodd Knutsen (Class of '59)

Brown Bullhead Ameiurus nebulosus

Losing Our Marbles — As soon as the warmth of the spring sun softened the dirt in our yards, we dug little holes about the size of a Campbell's soup can (tomato soup was the best) in the dirt so we could go out and play marbles. We scrambled around in our precious treasures drawer and dug out the marbles that we put away from last year. We counted them and sorted them…over and over. The more, the better; and the more colorful, the better. If you were really lucky, you had a few steelies.

Steelies were ball bearings… shiny silver balls of steel. With a steely, you could finger punch your friend's glass marble away from the hole, sink yours and win the game. And if you won, you got to keep his marbles. The mark of the marbles champ was the kid whose pockets bulged with marbles that he didn't have when he left the house, as he proudly walked his way slowly back home. **Bob Peters**

John Ryan's Pool — In the summer, Logan was a great place to hang around with friends. We'd ride our bikes over and just relax in the shade on hot summer days. It was a great gathering place.

For those of us who grew up in Lower Nordeast, the John Ryan swimming pool was the place to go. It was so exciting when I learned how to put my head underwater; I thought that was the coolest. I practiced swimming underwater until I could swim the length of the pool without coming up for air. We'd pay our

The Swimming Pool

(Continued on page 133)

(Continued from page 132)

dime and that would buy us an hour in the pool. The locker rooms and showers were on the main floor, and after changing one would go down several flights of stairs to get to the underground pool. I'm not sure how large the pool was, maybe 40' by 80'. I took my only formal swimming lessons there when I was 8.

The big negatives to the pool were the large amounts of chlorine they used and having to leave the water after an hour. But in the summer—it was off to the lakes! Lake Calhoun was a favorite before we had cars of our own. We could take public transportation. But as soon as some of my friends and I had our own cars, it was off to Lake Johanna. A hot summer day, a swim in Lake Johanna and lying around on the beach watching the girls; what a great summer life! **Louie Paff**

John Ryan's Locker Room
Image courtesy of the Minnesota Historical Society

La Tarantella

The Margaret Barry House — The main center of activity for us was the Margaret Barry House. It was located on Broadway and Pierce, one block behind our house. It was a settlement house for immigrants, which offered services for them. My family didn't really use any of the services, but I benefited from the kids' activities that took place every day after school. We had clubs, dancing lessons, crafts, cooking, sports, and music. At the end of the school year they would have a program for the parents. I remember learning to do the Tarantella, an Italian dance, for the pro-

(Continued on page 134)

(Continued from page 133)

gram.

favorite summer activity the Barry House offered was they took us to Camden Pool once or twice a week. It seems like we paid a nominal amount to go, like maybe a quarter. That paid for the bus ride and the swimming. We had a ball and it was an opportunity which we would never have gotten to swim in a pool.

Wayne Mandery, who ended up as my husband years later, went swimming and diving in high school and became high school swim coach as an adult.

I am sure that never would have happened had he not had the opportunity to learn to swim at Camden and at John Ryan's Pool, another pool near his house. **Sue Walker Mandery**

Camden Pool

The Knights — When we were in our early teens, we had a club called the Knights. Our "roundtable" headquarters was at the "Bughouse" the Margaret Barry House in Dogtown. Through the years, we have tried to get together at least once a year. **Bob Peters**

Good Times! — During this period we spent a lot of our time at the Margaret Barry House. Played basketball, shuffle board and formed a club called "The Knights." We had about 10 members. Always had a good time at the mistletoe dances at Christmas. **Ray Miller**

Bobby Peters & the Knights of the Round Table Front l-r Bob Peters, Ray Miller, Wayne Mandery Rear l-r Tom Krinke, Jim Moore, Jim McGuire

The Nut House — The Nut House is short for the Northeast Neighborhood House, a place where we as grade school kids would go after school and do supervised activities like gym, sewing/crafts, and cooking. We had a club for girls only and on Friday nights we had Canteen, which was for boys and girls. We met in a large room where we would play board games, cards, or just hang out. **Joanne Rau**

Curbing Ourselves — We played baseball in the street. Home plate was a manhole cover in the middle of the street. First base was a curb sewer on the right side of the street a little ways up. Second base was a manhole cover straight out in the center of the street. Third base was another curb sewer on the left-hand side of the street. The curbs, of course, were out of bounds. We used our Imagination…After supper, and until it got dark, we played Kick the Can and Hide and Seek. When it rained or got too hot, we read and traded comic books. The Classics were the ones everybody wanted, especially the Three Musketeers or Robinson Crusoe. Ahhh, quiet entertainment!
Bob Peters

Camping and Camaraderie — When I was 11, I joined Boy Scout Troop 77 at Emanuel Lutheran on 13th &Monroe. The troop was fabulous for me - the camping and the camaraderie. Many Point Scout Camp near Ponsford, MN, was a yearly highlight. We sometimes did weekend camping at Peck's Woods (just past the northeast edge of Columbia Heights). Now it's all housing. I made and strengthened wonderful friendships in the troop. Rod Nelson joined the troop shortly after I did. We went camping and did the other troop things, and we have a friendship that continues. The troop had two adult leaders who were wonderful influences on me. One was the scoutmaster, Neville Pearson. He was a prof at the U of MN, and he was a person devoted to helping young people grow in good ways. His kindly manner and wise counsel had a profound life changing influence on me. He is one of my heroes.

The other leader was our assistant scoutmaster, Hap Holstein. He was a full-blooded Ojibwa Indian, and he brought wonderful outdoors skills to scouting. Even more important he was able to give us confidence. One time I was supposed to do a mile long swim in Many Point Lake for advancement. I was sure I couldn't make it. I walked away from the lake. Hap spotted me, and asked, "Louie, why aren't you down at the lake?" I said, "Aw Hap, I know I can't swim a mile." He replied, "I know that you can. You get yourself down there and do it." And you know, I did swim that mile and felt so good about it afterward! He is another of my heroes. **Louie Paff**

Scout Camp

Front row l-r Rod Nelson, Dick Gulbranson, Louie Paff, Back row l-r Ron Lymer, Cliff Lee, John Skronick

CHAPTER-SEVEN — CLASS BACKWARDS

Family Life and Inventive Games

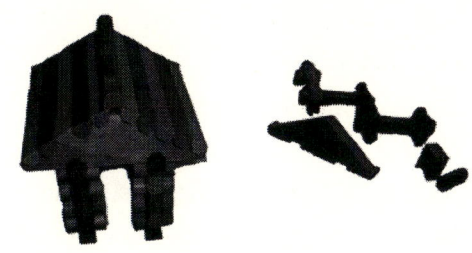

Holy Crap — Other indoor games challenged our imaginations for hours: Lincoln Logs, Tinker Toys and Erector Sets. Holy crap, some of the things I built actually went round and round. I smiled as I looked at my creation of the wheel! **Bob Peters**

Using Our Imagination — Board games and card games were played mostly by me, my younger sister, and brothers, although Mother could be coaxed to play at times. Dad never played any of them.

Some of earlier years were spent playing Old Maid or Go to the Dump for card games. Our favorite board Games as we grew older were checkers or Chinese Checkers, which you could keep playing as long as you didn't lose any of the pieces.

Coloring books, crayons, and wooden large piece puzzles developed our dexterity. Perhaps it was the smell of the crayons or the wood pieces that captured our attention and drew us into them. However, these arrived only during Christmas or maybe a birthday.

Games such as Go To The Head Of The Class, Pick Up Sticks, Monopoly, Operation, Parcheesi and Authors provided learning to be used later in life – though we didn't know it at the time. Tinker toys and the various contrap-

(Continued on page 138)

137

(Continued from page 137)

tions were set up alongside a wall to keep from being kicked over. The size was limited only by running out of pieces. Next year it was an Erector Set with motor and all. It worked best when you finally added the motor. I was not destined to be an engineer, but these two building kits, more than other activities, seemed to take me into another imaginative world while working or playing with them.

Plaster of Paris animals and other pieces plus figurine paints added to time-killers to keep us out of Mother's way while she kept the house and cleaned our clothes. Sometimes there could be a puzzle set up and worked on by all for hours or days until it was finished.

We invented games like jumping off the porch roof into the snow piles we shoveled. In the summer for tents we hung blankets over a clothesline with rocks holding down the corners.

And if you were lucky, you could climb the trees in your yard, only thinking about building a fort in it. In the spring with pools of melted snow and rivulets of water flowing everywhere in your yard or by the sidewalks, we built our own dams and created new rivers as we chopped drainage systems for melting ice to run away from the house.

Rod Nelson

CHAPTER-SEVEN **CLASS BACKWARDS**

Lights-Camera-Action — I remember a lot of games growing up. There were about a half dozen boys about my age on our block (bounded by 19th and 22nd Avenues and Garfield and Arthur Streets). Once we discovered each other, we'd play Cowboys and Indians or Cops and Robbers and other games all summer long. One girl our age (and some younger) lived on the block and they would often join in.

After breakfast, we'd report to mid-block at Paul Loebner's house to see what the day's schedule would be. Paul (Class of '59) had a vivid imagination and even in those pre-TV days, he went to movies a lot and spun great stories and plots for whatever was doing. Some were movie plots and some were strictly out of his imagination. He'd set the basic stage and we'd improvise from there. The day would often start with the group choice of the vehicle of the day: wagon, trike, or scooter. We'd ride those all around the block, using the sidewalks as cars would streets, driving by the rules, of course. Wagons would be propelled by kneeling in the wagon bed and pushing repetitively with the other leg.

For the staged games, of course, we needed guns. Except for some realistic looking silent revolvers, these took the form of cap guns in various styles, but we were collectively forbidden to use caps except around the 4th of July. Therefore, gunfire was vocally simulated. Of course, endless arguments ensued on who was shot and died and who hadn't.   **Bob Buntrock**

Nancy Drew Wannabes — Growing up, we relied on our imaginations to create drama. I remember when Kathleen Coveney and I played "detectives." She claimed she spotted a mysterious man putting a bloodied knife into his trunk by the 29th and Johnson Street drugstore. He drove off heading toward St. Anthony Village and we were convinced he was a dangerous man. So we walked almost a mile to where they were constructing new homes and saw a worker who looked kind of like the man at the drugstore. We started talking to him and went inside the house he was building. I took a picture of him with my Brownie camera when he entered the house. It didn't take long before we realized he probably wasn't the culprit and was just being nice to us by showing us what he was building. We became bored and finally left him alone.   **Carol Lyons Larson**

Small Spaces and Large Families — Living in Northeast Minneapolis in the mid 1940s and 1950s for me was all about family. The trend of the times was usually that extended family lived close by or in the same neighborhoods. With only one sister, I was lucky enough to be a part of and grow up in a large family of aunts, uncles, and cousins. There was always a reason for family gatherings. My mother had four brothers and three sisters who all loved celebrating birthdays, anniversaries, baptisms, first communions, or any other event, which my parents never missed. The fun part was that I, being one of the younger offspring, was able to experience adventures with plenty of cousins.

I remember, fondly, the birthday parties that took place at my grandma's house on 19th and Washington Street N.E. My grandfather, who died at an early age, would have been proud of his wife, Susie, for her spirit of family that she gave to all of us. She had a small house with very little room for the kids to play. Of course, there were no electronic devices like the children have today to keep us occupied. We had to create ways to entertain ourselves with each other using our imagination in a house where 25-30 people gathered in a small living room and dining room. The older cousins played board games in a small side bedroom.

(Continued on page 142)

(Continued from page 141)

In the winter months, the favorite spot for four of us younger kids to play, where no grown-ups were allowed, was under Grandma's BIG dining room table with the heavy chairs. It was the perfect place to get out of the way of the preparations of the celebration and have just the right spot. From under the table, peeking through the lace tablecloth, we would think we were in an enchanted place. Maybe a castle or a house made out of ice with the lace reminding us of little snowflakes on our windows. Sometimes the boys pretended it was a scary cave.

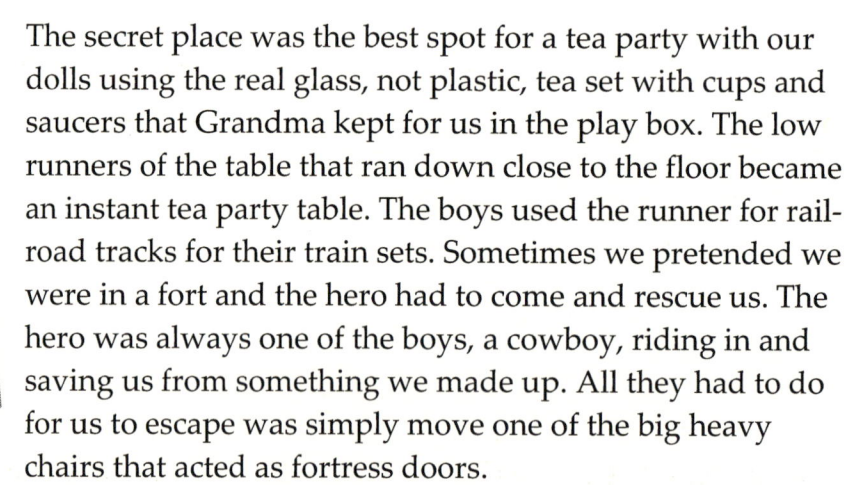

The secret place was the best spot for a tea party with our dolls using the real glass, not plastic, tea set with cups and saucers that Grandma kept for us in the play box. The low runners of the table that ran down close to the floor became an instant tea party table. The boys used the runner for railroad tracks for their train sets. Sometimes we pretended we were in a fort and the hero had to come and rescue us. The hero was always one of the boys, a cowboy, riding in and saving us from something we made up. All they had to do for us to escape was simply move one of the big heavy chairs that acted as fortress doors.

Under the table was also a good place to play checkers or Old Maid because the adults would not have to step over us or disturb our pieces. Tinker Toy creations made this lit-

(Continued on page 143)

(Continued from page 142)

tle space into anything we wanted. We could hear our parents and older cousins laughing and talking loudly as they played cards or just sat around. They would not forget that we were in our little make-believe world under the table, or so we thought. They would say, "Where are the little kids?" Then the game became Hide and Seek with our very own perfect hiding spot. I wonder why they could never find us?

Grandma knew exactly where to look when it was time for the "special person" to blow out the birthday candles. We wasted no time leaving our play place to get a piece of her yummy banana layered white cake topped with fluffy white frosting. All the adults and children would gather around the long table to sing, "Happy Birthday." After we ate our cake, we would sometimes all stand around the piano singing songs and maybe dancing with the grown-ups. Since there wasn't a playroom or game room for all of us to spread out in, I think their motive was to get the wiggles out of 5 and 6-year-olds by dancing around.

We would then forget all about our secret spot under the table, of course, until the next special celebration at Grandma's little house. It has always been warm to my heart to have such wonderful memories growing up in a small community with many relatives who lived so close to us. Sharing family gatherings in a small space will always remain one of the joys of my life. **Marilyn Sexton Lubrecht**

CLASS BACKWARDS

CHAPTER-SEVEN

CHAPTER EIGHT:
THAT'S ENTERTAINMENT?

Movies in the '40s were stories that featured adults (with a few exceptions like *The Wizard of Oz*, *National Velvet* or the *Andy Hardy* series). Many of us spent hours of our lives with our friends and members of our families at theaters. "They were the stuff that dreams were made of..." When at home, we gathered around the radio and used our imaginations. At the end of the era, drive-in movies became popular and families would attend them in their family car. A strange new invention called television was becoming part of our evening's entertainment. During the warm summer nights, we all became performers as neighborhoods came together at local parks like Windom, sang songs, and listened to Elmo Lunkley's band. Computers? Never heard of 'em.

The Movies

The Arion — Does anyone remember the movie theater on Central Avenue? I remember it cost five cents to get in and I think popcorn was ten cents. We used to go to the Matinees on Saturday and Sunday afternoons.

Other times we would go up the hill to the Hollywood movie theater but that also cost ten cents.
Bev Decker-Johnson

Whata Deal — My sisters used to work the ticket booth at the Arion Theater and I got in free until I was about 8. Every Saturday we saw serials, and Westerns with John Wayne.
Tom Urista.

The Ritz — Every Sunday afternoon hordes of kids would go to watch the movie of the week at the Ritz Theater on 13th Avenue between 4th Street and University. It was 12 cents for the ticket and my parents always gave me another nickel to buy a box of popcorn. In later years the cost rose to 25 cents and then to 50 cents – too expensive to go every week.

It was a meeting place for so many of us. My girlfriends and I would sit in one row and the boys would sit one or two rows behind us. We knew we were in for teasing, poking, pulling hair and an occasional

(Continued on page 147)

(Continued from page 146)

empty popcorn box sailing through the air and landing on our heads or our shoulders. We even tried to get angry and tell them to stop it to no avail. As I think back, it was fun to be noticed, even if it was being noticed by those mean boys.

When the lights went down, the show began with a newsreel, cartoon and an episode of a serial. We had to go each week to see if the cowboy really fell over the cliff, or if the bad guys really shot our hero. Sometimes we even watched the movie.
Carolyn Jodie Hagford

Noisy Kids — The Ritz Theater was another place I spent some time. I loved movies and usually attended the Saturday and Sunday matinee. The theater on Saturday was full of noisy kids eating popcorn and candy, getting more wound up than ever. The cowboy movies with the likes of Roy Rogers, Gene Autry, and Hop-a-Long Cassidy were very popular as were the comedies with Abbott and Costello and, of course, Laurel and Hardy—my favorites. Sunday the theater had adults attending as well as youngsters so the theater was a little more subdued.
Jean Torgerson Strong

Scary Fun — I was fascinated by the movies and so I often sat through the movie twice, even double features. There was a period of time when my favorite place to sit was the front row. The candy of choice had to be a Holloway sucker, Bit o' Honey, or a box of Milk Duds—never popcorn. Once I sat through the mystery movie, covering my ears and eyes at the scary parts. It ended in early evening so it was getting dark. I was about eight and had to walk—rather run as fast as I could—the four blocks home. Even at home I was so scared that I went to my bed by keeping my back against the wall. I don't do that much any more! **Rod Nelson**

The Hollywood — I loved going to the movies at an early age (usually the Hollywood Theater on 28th and Johnson.) My favorite actors were Roy Rogers and the Sons of the Pioneers. Gabby Hayes didn't do much for me.

I used to think I sounded like Judy Garland and that I was going to be a movie star someday so toward that end, formed a neighborhood theater group the ACME Players. It was composed of Audrey, Carol, Meg (my cousin) and Elsa. We would put on plays in Elsa's garage until one day Meg hit Elsa's brother over the head with one of the props and that closed down our theater. **Carol Lyons Larson**

CHAPTER · EIGHT   **CLASS BACKWARDS**

The Westerns — I remember going to the Hollywood Theatre. We would walk the six blocks or so to see the Saturday matinee – often a western preceded by the *Movietone News* and one or more cartoons if we were lucky. And only for a dime - then the outrageous price of 12 cents. On the way home we would reenact the movie – especially if it was a western. **Dick Myslajek**

Three views of the interior of the old Hollywood Theater as it appeared in our youth
Photos courtesy of Cinema Treasures http://cinematreasures.org/

My Reel Life — In the beginning '50s I was voluntarily held captive in a darkened room for seven and a half hours both Saturday and Sunday, with only a Holloway sucker to sustain me. What a deal! For 17 cents, including the sucker, I was transfixed for the entire afternoon. The only drawback was that occasionally I had to bring my dopey kid sister along. Every good thing has its price.

The building was the Hollywood Theater, on the Bryant-Johnson streetcar line. It is now being considered for renovation as a prime example of the *art deco* style, which makes me laugh because none of my movie-going friends had much style. The din in the theater resembled a locust attack, with everyone yelling to each other, the screen, and to themselves.

There were two features, a *Pathe News*, a *Masked Marvel* adventure serial featuring a lumpy super hero in dress pants, a Joe McDoakes comedy in which Joe screwed up everything he tried, and maybe five

(Continued on page 151)

(Continued from page 150)

cartoons. My favorite features were the mysteries: *Charlie Chan*, *the Falcon*, and *Bulldog Drummond*. Sometimes I would be distracted by details. For instance, the Falcon's cigarette never seemed to burn down, and he never slept, but I would overlook the fact he was always alone and never seemed to have any friends. My shoes might be stuck to the gum-varnished floor, but my mind was also stuck on unraveling the *Secret of the Lone Wolf*.

When I left the theater I was pretty much ruined. After the show, I trudged home along the streets. I really didn't want to leave the colorful world of dramatic darkness for my beige existence. The reel life trivialized my real life.

Red Lyons, class of '55

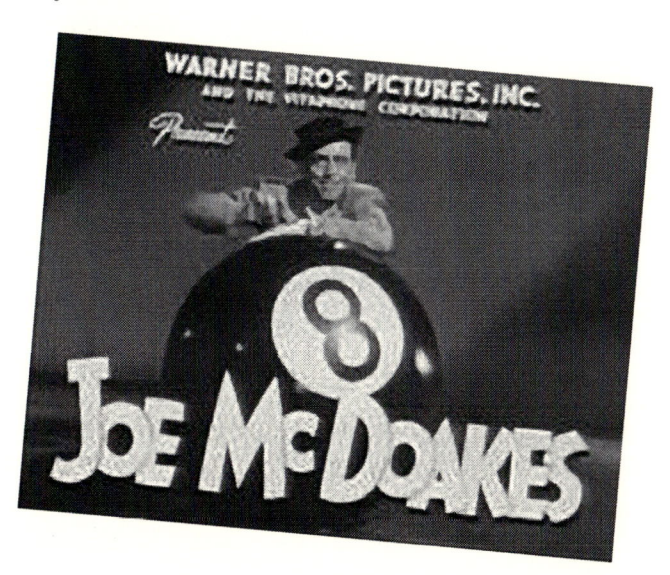

CLASS BACKWARDS — CHAPTER EIGHT

The Drive-Ins — I became aware of drive-in movies in the late 1940's when my parents loaded the whole family into the car — a Frazer manufactured sometime after 1946. Even the phrase "after the war" indicates the geriatric nature of the memory. We kids, dressed in our pajamas, would take our pillows and one blanket and settle into the back seat of the car. Once through the ticket booth, we had to pick a spot to park and then pull the speaker into the car and hang it on the window.

Post War Frazer (probably 1947)

Obviously, drive-ins in Minnesota did not operate all year long. Drive-in season began in late spring and ran through early fall. Even then, the weather might be cool and the people sitting next to the speaker window would be bothered by a constant cool draft. Usually, however, it was on a summer evening with the ever present Minnesota pest buzzing in our ears. Just before the films would start, a truck drove back and forth between the rows of cars shooting out a cloud of DDT or some other insecticide.

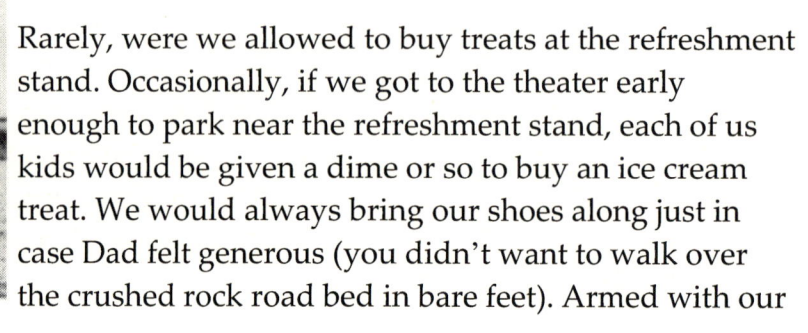

Rarely, were we allowed to buy treats at the refreshment stand. Occasionally, if we got to the theater early enough to park near the refreshment stand, each of us kids would be given a dime or so to buy an ice cream treat. We would always bring our shoes along just in case Dad felt generous (you didn't want to walk over the crushed rock road bed in bare feet). Armed with our

(Continued on page 153)

(Continued from page 152)

treats, our pillows, and our blanket, we'd settle down to watch the movie. In those days, no matter what age group the film was aimed at, they would show a cartoon before the feature film. The cartoon was easy to pay attention to, but often, the feature film didn't make any sense to us and I remember trying desperately to stay awake just to prove how adult I was. But even when our parents had picked a good film – translate that as a western – the time of day would do me in.
Larry Kohout

Radio Imagination — Some of my best memories from growing up are about sitting around or driving with my family listening to the radio. "The Lone Ranger" with its great music was so exciting, and when we later got television and I saw it there, it was such a disappointment. What they put on TV couldn't measure up to the Lone Ranger that I had been imagining in my head. Edgar Bergen and Charlie McCarthy were funny, even though it's strange to think of ventriloquists being on the radio. It seems to lose the point,

(Continued on page 154)

(Continued from page 153)
but it didn't make any difference to me. I loved them. Then there was "The Shadow." I mostly remember the theme line, "Who knows what evil lurks in the hearts of men? The Shadow knows." There was also "The Green Hornet" and many more that I don't remember. It was a great chance to use my imagination, and television never quite measured up to what I had seen in my head. **Norm Solberg**

The Glow in the Night — On top of the refrigerator sat a Bakelite Coronado radio that my dad would listen to sports events in the evenings. It was such a scratchy, crackly radio, and I grew to hate the sound of it.

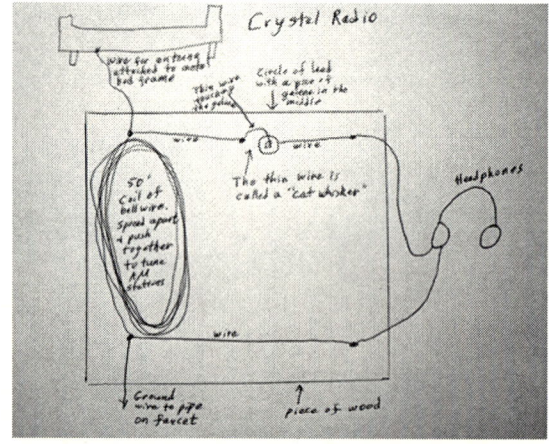

Louies's diagram of his crystal set

But I was interested in electronics, so I first built a crystal radio, crude, but it worked fine. I used the metal frame of my hideaway bed for an antenna. Then I built a one tube radio using a hearing aid tube from a neighbor across the hall. Hard to believe that hearing aids at one time had electron tubes. They were called sub-miniature, but were about 3/16 inches thick by 5/16 inches wide by about 2 inches long. I used that radio at night after I was supposed to be asleep. My mother could see the glow of the filament from the bedroom and would tell me to turn it off. So I slipped a paper roll over the tube to cover the glow, and from then on I could listen to the radio as late as I wanted. **Louie Paff**

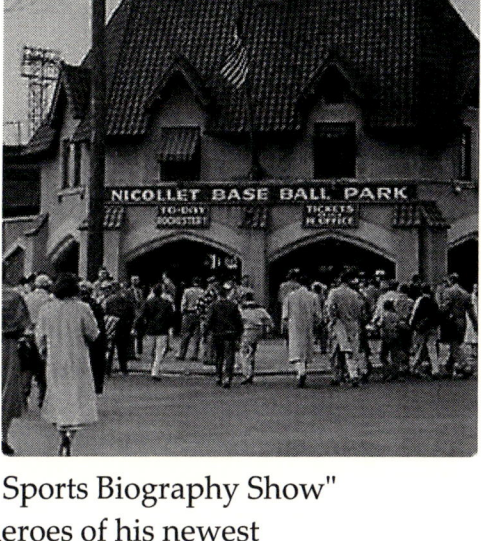

Tuning to a Past Gone Forever — Listening to the radio stretched our creativity and our imaginations. I have fond memories of my mom, in our kitchen, listening to her favorite soap opera as she stirred up a batch of cookies. (From scratch, of course.)

My dad would be smoking his cigar in our living room with all the lights turned off, listening to the Millers' ball game broadcasted from Nicollet Stadium. My brother and I oooohed as Bill Stern on the "Colgate Sports Biography Show" finally divulged the heroes of his newest story.

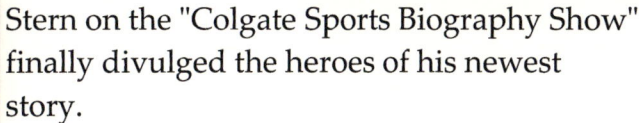

And on Saturdays, I would play with my Shirley Temple paper dolls, sit on the floor by the radio with my family home for the morning, listen to Smilin' Ed McConnell's program about Buster Brown who lived in a shoe with his dog, Tighe, that lived in there too. **Carol Lyons Larson**

Songs You Could Sing — My mother always had the radio on while I grew up. There was a soft background of tunes that even today I am surprised that I can still sing along with as well as place myself back to that age and the memories rekindled by the particular song. In the evening she would switch to comedy shows or Your Hit Parade. Never did we listen to mysteries. Too scary. Of course, later Cedric Adams and the news always bid us goodnight. **Rod Nelson**

The Inner Sanctum — The radio was a great way to spend cold winter nights. I can still hear the "Squeaking Door" and shaking as I listened to "The Inner Sanctum." I laughed at the antics of "Amos and Andy" and thrilled to the adventures of the "Lone Ranger" and "Gene Autry."
Bobby Peters

Television

Test Pattern — I have to laugh when I remember staring at the screens of the first television sets in our neighborhood. We would watch "test patterns" which were made up of geometric shapes that would change every minute or so, accompanied by music in the background. We were so easily entertained. **Carol Lyons Larson**

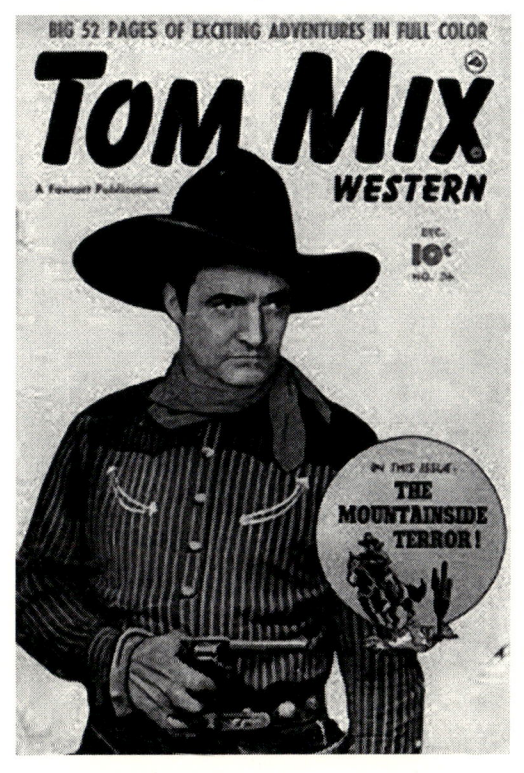

Our First TV Set — About 1949-50, one of our neighbors got a TV. It was in a m1ahogany wood cabinet and was probably about a 12-14 inch model. His name was Bill Diehl and he lived in a double bungalow on Lowry between Cleveland and Benjamin. He and his wife were in the beginning stages of starting a radio station which I think was the forerunner to KTIS. It was a semi-religious station located on Stinson Boulevard. He went on to become very successful and well known. They would invite some of the neighborhood kids to come in and watch TV, a very nice gesture on their part. The programs that I remember were Howdy-Doody and some westerns like Hopalong Cassidy and Tom Mix. It was such an amazing thing to watch these fuzzy black and white TV shows. They motivated us kids to go home and badger our parents to get TVsets.

My sisters and I pestered my dad and finally he relented in

(Continued on page 158)

CLASS BACKWARDS — CHAPTER EIGHT

(Continued from page 157)

about 1950-51 and got us a TV set. He worked for Midland Co-op located on Broadway and Johnson. Midland was a wholesale co-op that supplied farmer co-ops around the state with petroleum, farm supplies and merchandise. So we were able to get our TV at a wholesale price. I have the vague recollection that it cost a couple of hundred dollars, which was a huge sum. As a reference point, my dad had purchased a new 1947 Plymouth car for $750 in late 1947. This TV was about a 15-inch model. It received the signal from a rabbit ears antenna. The picture was supposed to be black and white but some stations were more like a fuzzy grey and white. We had two or three stations and you had to adjust the rabbit ears antenna whenever you changed stations. There were no remote controls so, to change stations, we had to go to the TV set and change the dial. It functioned using about 12 to 15 various vacuum tubes inside the cabinet but accessible to the homeowner. Quite frequently some of these tubes would become weak or burn out. We would have to pull them out of their sockets and go to the drug store in St. Anthony Village where they had a testing machine. We would purchase the replacement tubes and return home to fix the TV and with great excitement and watch our favorite shows including Groucho Marx and Friday night boxing matches.

John Vandermyde

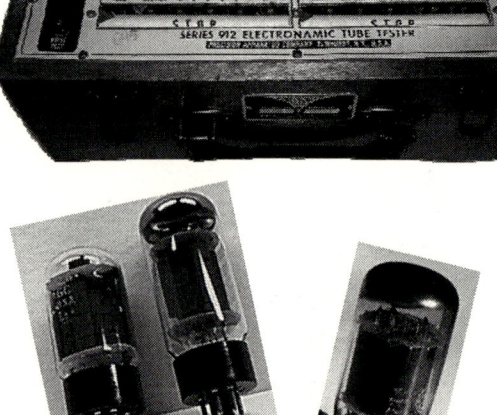

Pandora's Box — I grew up listening to evocative, creative radio shows that released my unbounded senses, because there were no boundaries to what I could imagine. Then, in 1947 my dad set up a television box, 7 by 9 inches. It featured sporting events that appeared to have been played in a London fog and programs like *Captain Video* that looked like they were shot by Junior High adolescents for an English project, but I never returned to radio again.

Today, the size of television sets has grown exponentially and can still expand our imagination... but only to the size of the screen. **Red Lyons Class of '55**

Living The Life of Riley — In the year 1949, my grandparents bought a television set. My sister and I snuck down there any chance we could. "Howdy-Doody" was the rage on TV, with Buffalo Bob and Princess Summer-Fall-Winter-Spring entertaining kids across the country.

At the age of 10, my parents built a house and we sorely missed the TV. So, one evening my Dad announced that we were all going shopping. I remember going to a furniture store on East Hennepin Avenue where a man from our church was the salesperson. We bought the most beautiful Muntz Console TV.

Our house was only 2 blocks from our church. On Monday evenings, at 6:00 PM, we walked there for Junior Choir Re-

(Continued on page 160)

(Continued from page 159)

hearsal. On the way home, we RAN in order to not miss the beloved "I Love Lucy Show" beginning at 7:00 PM.

We had our favorite cowboy shows: The Lone Ranger and Hopalong Cassidy, our brain testing shows: Twenty Questions, and just plain fun shows: Life of Riley and Amos and Andy.

It seems as though we had a better selection back then with only a few channels than we do now with 100 plus. Or is it that we choose to remember how fun life was when things were "simple"? **Bobby Peters**

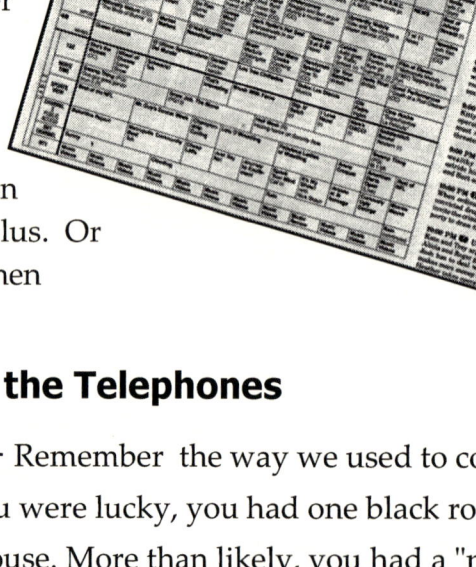

Don't Forget the Telephones

Ringy-Dingy — Remember the way we used to contact each other? If you were lucky, you had one black rotary telephone in your house. More than likely, you had a "party line" which meant you had to share a line with your neighbor. To call someone, you had to use your finger to input their number in a circular dial. And if you were especially lucky, your party line was having an interesting conversation you could overhear. **Carol Lyons Larson**

| CHAPTER · EIGHT | CLASS BACKWARDS |

Band—Choir Concerts

The Big Show — During the '40s, music was valued by the community. The big show for the Sheridan community was the Spring Band and Choir Concert. A grade school "B" band played, various choirs sang, and then the "A" Jr. High band with its traditional "military" drum and bugle entrance marching down the aisles.

We spent days knocking on doors to sell the tickets. The sales were by rooms and motivated by a contest. The result was an evening in the gym/auditorium filled with neighbors and family members. The stage

Chuck Grissom and Lou Paff modeling Red Owl Uniforms for Aquatennial Parade

(Continued on page 162)

The 1949 combined Sheridan Band & Choir

(Continued from page 161)

was decorated and had a front line of lilacs that always seemed to be in bloom at the time. After the concert of well played and sung pieces, we'd head home. My family always had root beer floats awaiting us. Probably the only time we had them. We felt proud to wear the band's green and white uniforms. Some are still in existence as costumes at Minneapolis Southwest High School. Some members then joined and played in the Henry High Red Owl band for the Aquatennial.
Rod Nelson

The 'In' Place To Be — The biggest days of the summer at our park (Windom) were Tuesdays. During late June, July and early August it was "Band Concert Day." A Park Board truck would come around noon and drop off the song sheets and equipment for that night. A man would come and spray the park with DDT. Kids were all over the park and we got sprayed along with the trees and the grass-I don't think any of us died from the exposure. Hundreds of people came to enjoy the evening including families and high school and grade school students galore from Pillsbury, Lowry, Waite Park, Prescott and Edison High School. It was the "in" place to be. The popcorn wagon was parked on 23rd by the tennis courts. It was a 1930s Ford and had the best popcorn and cream soda in town.

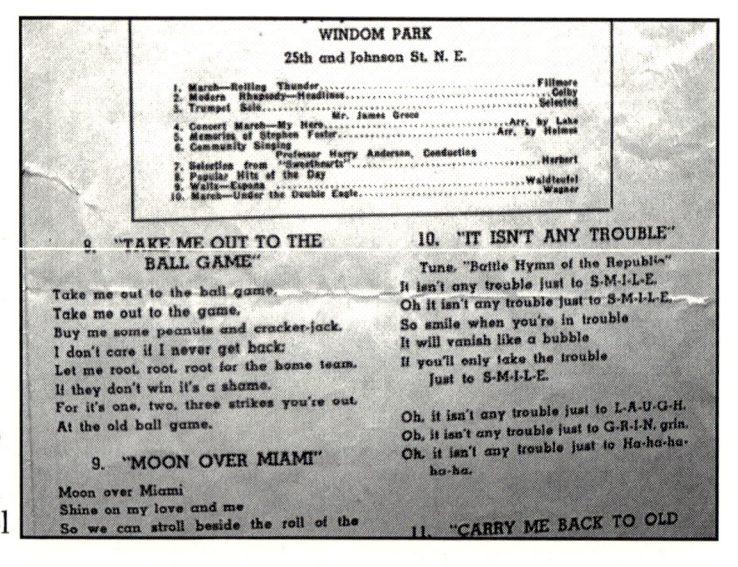

(Continued on page 163)

CHAPTER EIGHT   CLASS BACKWARDS

(Continued from page 162)

The Gopher State Concert Band was the entertainment and the bandleader was Elmo Lunkley, the band teacher at Edison High School for about 30 years. They played five nights a week around the city at various parks including Powderhorn on Wednesday, North Commons on Thursday, and Logan on Friday. Windom usually won the trophy for the best crowds and participation each year and they were displayed at the drug store on 22nd and Johnson.

The band of about 35 to 40 was actually very good and would play a number of musical selections and that was followed by State Rep. George Murk leading the sing-along.
Al, the guy who handed out the music sheets, usually was brought up on the bandstand and he sang a song-not very good, but he was entertaining. I don't think any of the kids were very involved because they were busy in their little groups talking and making moves on each other. Two different bandstands were at Windom. The first was at the high point in the park near Lowry and Johnson and it burned and was replaced by a concrete structure in the middle of the park near the pump with the best well water. It was a money-maker all summer for us pumping the water for people with gallon jugs. But our best money maker was the next morning after the band concert. We came early with flashlights and combed the grass in front of the bandstand for the change that fell out of people's pockets while they were sitting on the ground during the concert. The second best site was where the popcorn wagon was on 23rd. That was usually worth a few bucks. We hung at the park for many years, but when we got our driver's license, it was "Adios Amigos" except for Tuesdays. That was Band Concert Day!!
Gordie Solz

163

CLASS BACKWARDS — CHAPTER EIGHT

Top Ten Dumb Things We Thought Would Be Entertaining

#1 Crawling — We had wooden open stairs leading to our root cellar in the basement. When I was in first grade, I decided to crawl between the steps. My head got stuck and I started to cry. I yelled for my mom and dad, and they assured me they would get me out, discussing if they should saw me out. Then my mom coached me about not trying to force my way through, but to twist my head gently, and gradually I was able to push myself out of a very tight situation. **Carol Lyons Larson**

#2 Twisting — Twisting up the tire swing, then hanging in it while it spun to untwist, thinking of chow mein, and then getting sick. **Rod Nelson**

#3 Sticking to a Flagpole — That flagpole in Thomas Lowry's School yard was just standing there, waiting to be touched on a cold, wintry day. I had heard advice not to do this, but I stuck out my tongue and licked it anyway. I ended up with a bloody tongue as a hard lesson. I should've listened to the warnings. **Carol Lyons Larson**

164

CHAPTER EIGHT   CLASS BACKWARDS

#4 Rocking — At age 5, one of the dumbest things I did was to stand up in our big rocking chair as I was looking over its back while rocking as hard as I could. It tipped over backwards and I am reminded of it every day of my life by the tiny scar on my forehead. Of course, I was told not to do it by my parents because I might get hurt. A teachable moment. **Marilyn Sexton Lubrecht**

#5 Getting Nailed — Dumbest thing I ever did as a kid - there's lots of options ;-) I'd say it occurred during the summer when I was 6 or so. I had a balsa wood glider outdoors that I was enjoying throwing. It got stuck in a branch of an elm tree. To get it down I picked up small pieces of concrete from a nearby construction site and in turn threw them at the glider. My mistake was in running under the tree to gather the pieces before the last one came down. How stupid that was! The last one nailed me on my forehead right at the scalp line. It hurt like crazy and bled freely. So I went running for my mom who of course made it all better as only moms can do at that age. **Louie Paff**

165

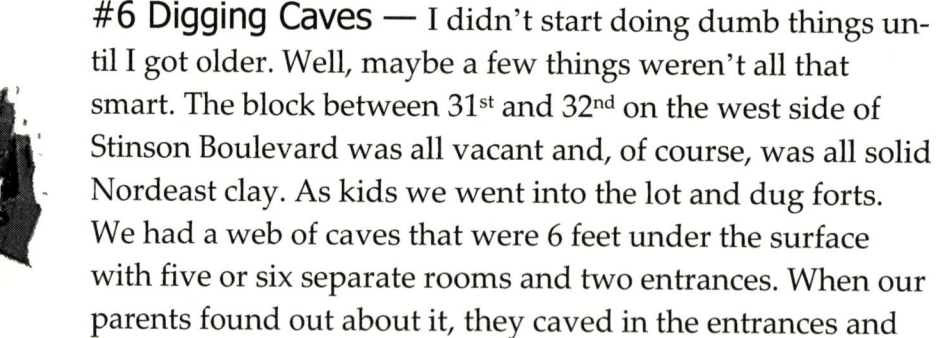

#6 Digging Caves — I didn't start doing dumb things until I got older. Well, maybe a few things weren't all that smart. The block between 31st and 32nd on the west side of Stinson Boulevard was all vacant and, of course, was all solid Nordeast clay. As kids we went into the lot and dug forts. We had a web of caves that were 6 feet under the surface with five or six separate rooms and two entrances. When our parents found out about it, they caved in the entrances and forbid us to do anything like that again. In my late teens, I was sitting on our back porch watching the driver of a bull dozer digging the foundation for the last new house to complete that block. He had just started to push the earth around when the machine suddenly dropped about 4 feet into the earth. The driver leaped from the machine in a panic, and for a minute or two I was puzzled about what had happened. It then dawned on me that the old caves were right under where he was digging. I don't know what our parents were concerned about. It took a 6-ton bull dozer to break into our caves. **Larry Kohout**

#7 Drowning — On a hot afternoon, at the end of sixth grade, my friend Barbara and I decided to go to Lake Harriet to swim. We could get on the Johnson Street streetcar and ride to the end of the line and walk a few blocks and there we were at the lake. I had done this before with another friend

(Continued on page 167)

CHAPTER EIGHT — CLASS BACKWARDS

(Continued from page 166)

and we had had a lot of fun.

Barb wasn't sure if she wanted to go even if I had said it would be fun. She had two good reasons: her hesitation was due to the fact that she could not swim and she was frightened of the water.

I was not a good swimmer either, but I was not afraid of the water. My parents had taken me to many lakes in Minnesota, so I was very comfortable around water.

I got Barb to go in the lake; however, she was not comfortable at all. We were fooling around and splashing one another. We were further out in the water than we realized. Suddenly I was under Barb.

She panicked and froze and did not move and she actually had me trapped under her body. It all happened so quickly I couldn't believe I found myself in this position. My life flashed before me and I was sure I would be dead if I did not move this object.

I thought to myself I am too young to die. I either bit or pinched Barb to get her to move. Lo and behold that worked. To this day I feel that if she had not moved that minute I wouldn't be writing this today. Thank God she moved!!

Jean Togerson Strong

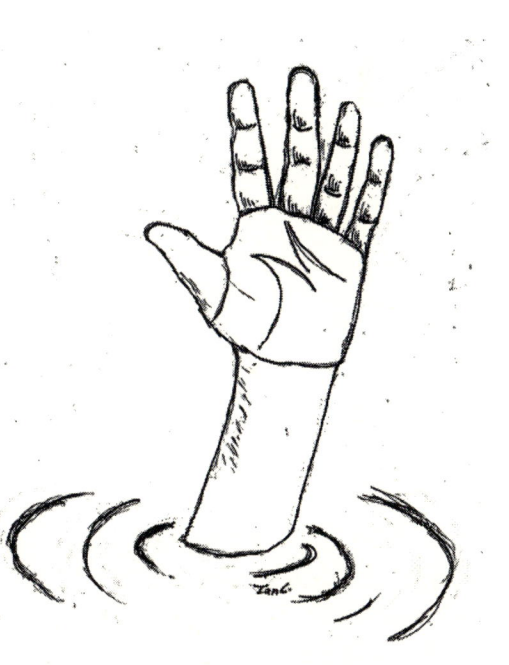

#8 Rocketing — Ah yes, dumb kid things as a kid…I do remember several daring stunts that fortunately didn't lead to injury or worse. Some were associated with my basement chemistry laboratory and other explosives capers with friends. A notable series of potential incidents involved finding, with a friend and classmate, discarded ReddiWhip cans in the dumping area a block below my house. We'd build a fire and put the cans in. If pointed upright, the nozzle would eventually blow straight up in the air for 20 feet or so. A couple of times, we'd put the can in upside down and the nozzle would melt first before exploding, propelling the entire can around like a rocket. Through pure dumb luck, we never got hit with any of these missiles. **Bob Buntrock**

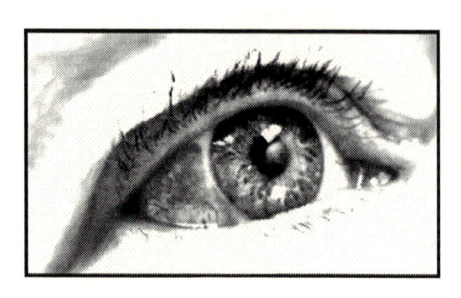

#9 Hemorrhaging — Night time was for "kick the can" and "hide and go seek." One of those nights, my twin sister Janice ran out from behind a garage and ran smack into Dick Hager (class of '55) and split her head open above the eye, off to the hospital for stitches. Forever after Mr. Jorgenson, our art teacher at Lowry, called her "Ruby Eyeball" as her eye hemorrhaged and stayed bright red for a long time.
Judy Sheldon Johnson

#10 Sneaking — Joey Godava, Frankie Burmis and I used to walk downtown to the Radio City or State movie theaters and try to sneak in without paying. Most of the time, we were successful. In colder weather, we would take off our coats, hang around the lobby for a few minutes, and buy a bag of popcorn so it looked like we had been there before. Then it was easy to walk back in. One time, however, we got caught in Radio City Theater and the police were called. They told us we were going to be arrested and scared the living daylights out of us. Then, when they saw how scared we were, they told us they would let us go just this one time. We learned our lesson! After that, we only snuck into the State Theater.
Jerry Kondrak

Lobby of the Radio City Theater
Can you find Jerry, Joey, and Frankie?

CLASS BACKWARDS

CHAPTER · EIGHT

CHAPTER NINE:
GRADE SCHOOLS

"I pledge allegiance to the flag of the United States of America, and to the republic for which it stands, one nation, indivisible, with liberty and justice for all."

With our hands on our hearts and facing the flag, every morning we started school with this salute. The many hours spent away from home were mainly spent in elementary school somewhere in our neighborhood. Some of us remember crying as we entered school away from our home, but once we adjusted, there was a feeling of solidarity to our classrooms. Desks were fastened to the floor in straight rows. We marched out to recess in orderly lines. We took good care of our books. Our school days were shorter then, taking time for a long recess and going home for lunch. We were taught to always show respect for our teachers, but sometimes substitutes were fair game. Paper sales and circuses were major events. Stories still linger of those days in elementary school and on the playground...

PILLSBURY

We Made It Work — My first day in kindergarten, some girl wouldn't share blocks to play with so I ran home crying. My mother had to calm me down and walk me back.

Waite Park under construction
Courtesy of the Minnesota Historical Society

Central Avenue Library of the 1940s & '50s

By fifth grade, Pillsbury had an enrollment decrease because Waite Park School had been finished. Earlier in the '40s, Carey School had burned and Cavell had been closed. This dumped a bunch of Cavell kids on Pillsbury and Lowry who now had a new grade school of their own. As a result, there were only enough kids for 1½ sections of both fifth and sixth graders, so two half-sections of each grade were combined and I was in that class. (Doug Tanner, Edison '57 was in there too.) Mrs. Larson was the teacher and along with us we managed to make it work. If we got our class work done on time, she'd read to us. Not just anything, but *Little House on the Prairie, Mary Poppins, Caddie Woodlawn,* and other soon-to-be classics. She'd tease us by reading just the first book in a series and encourage us to borrow the others and read them if interested. This always prompted a mad rush to the Central Avenue Library to be the first to check out the next book. **Bob Buntrock**

CHAPTER NINE — CLASS BACKWARDS

First Grade Memories — Kindergarten passed in a haze– probably most of my school years passed in a haze as I was anything but a student – and I was shuttled off to Pillsbury for grades one through four. But Pillsbury was eight long blocks south and six short blocks west of us. So my educational career continued with busing. A bus to school in the morning, a bus home for lunch, another bus back to school for the afternoon, and the final ride at the end of the day. When a quarter century later a system of busing to achieve racial diversity was started, it seemed to me like the normal thing that went along with school.

Pillsbury School of the 1940s & '50s

My first day of first grade started on a cool and rainy fall day. The bus pulled up alongside Pillsbury, and I still hold a memory of the school lit like a Christmas tree. But in order to get from the bus to the school, we had to cross a gravel yard through the rain and in our squeaking black rain coats and hats.

I was assigned to Mrs. Murphy's first grade class. Now how would I remember that 63 years later? Mrs. Murphy, like all the teachers I had through those first four years, was a gentle but firm disciplinarian. I worked like the devil to try and get myself out of the lowest reading group. Looking back now I suspect I probably had/have dyslexia or something of the like. I so wanted to get into that group with Bob Buntrock and some of the other leaders, but I could never quite make it. I did manage the middle group by the end of the year. But that was only the beginning. After reading we had to confront numbers! **Larry Kohout**

173

CLASS BACKWARDS — CHAPTER · NINE

School Grounds — There was a lawn at the front of the school which was off-limits for playing, winter or summer. One winter day, several kids took advantage of a fresh snowfall and built forts. They had to be destroyed and some sort of reprimand was meted out. The half-block to the south of school was always graveled and the area to the back was initially graveled. At some time, the remainder of the area around the school was asphalted which eliminated a large area for playing marbles in the spring. The tradeoff was that four basketball baskets were placed on the north and south walls. They were about 7-8 feet high so several of the taller kids could dunk.

Recess was always popular. Games like Tag, Red Rover, and Duck, Duck Gray Duck were played in the fall. During the winter we played Pie. We tramped out a wheel with eight-spokes in the snow and the only safe spot was in the middle, occupied by one person only. If you were tagged, you were It. In the spring, there was a mad dash to the ball diamond. The first out (usually Gordy Solz and friends) got to choose the order for Two Batter Scrub. If you were too far down the list, you never got a chance to bat. Ball was played after school and on weekends too. There was a relatively short left field fence which, although two cyclone sections high, could often surrender a home run by the "Big Kids.." Since there was a

(Continued on page 175)

CHAPTER NINE   CLASS BACKWARDS

(Continued from page 174)

house and yard back of that section of fence, the neighbors weren't too happy about it and complained. The principal laid down the law: any hit over that fence was an out.

We commenced with pride at the end of sixth grade and traded in our BMOC status the next fall for puny peon status as seventh graders at Edison. What a comedown!
Bob Buntrock

Grammar Matters — In fifth grade we were asked to write a paper about what we did over Easter Vacation (now spring break.) My teacher sent the paper home to my parents with a phrase underlined and wanted to know if they knew what I'd been doing during vacation. The phrase said that I had been "making dames down by the sewer."

I still subscribe to Mark Twain's outlook on spelling: It is a terribly dull individual who only knows one way to spell a word. **Larry Kohout**

Edith Cavell

A Famous Visitor — The first school I attended was Edith Cavell, an old white-painted wooden building located on the 3400 block between Fillmore and Pierce Streets. Lindy, the custodian for the school, was a friendly fellow who tolerated us quite well. At the start of the school Lindy would go out on the front porch of the school and ring a bell notifying us that school was about to begin. At times he would let us ring the bell.

One winter some of us were caught throwing snowballs and were marched through the closest outside door which was into a sixth grade classroom. Quite embarrassing. I know my parents were not amused when they received the call from the principal. Cavell School was demolished in 1947. After the demolition part of the block was set aside for the kids to build little shacks. The site was called Yardville. You were assigned a plot of ground on which to build your little building. President Truman visited the site one day. When the president was leaving, we ran with the motorcade up to Johnson Street and south on Johnson Street until they sped away.

Dodd Knutsen (Class of '56)

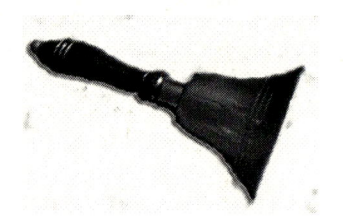

President Truman waves his hat to the crowd

CHAPTER · NINE CLASS BACKWARDS

Bell Bottom Trousers — Some of my fondest memories of school were of Edith Cavell School. It was an old one story white wooden building with small classrooms and a large main hallway which served as a gym and auditorium. What is strange is that I only physically attended Edith Cavell for a few days. I started there in fourth grade, but after a few days my class was moved to an overflow facility, a small chapel on 33rd and Pierce Street. That was the last year the school was open, replaced by Waite Park. My first memory — before I was old enough to start school — was attending a student show with my mother, and being very impressed with the students singing "Bell Bottom Trousers." It was during World War II. For some reason it is still imprinted in my memory.
Dick Myslajek

Thomas Lowry

Thomas Lowry of the '40s and '50s

A Doomed Romance — In our younger years we used to walk home from Lowry Grade School to have lunch. Many times, I would walk with my first girlfriend, Carol Lyons. When I would get a chance, I would give her a hip check (a hockey term) upsetting her balance. Most of this was in fun, but sometimes it annoyed her.

One day she went home and asked her mother, "Why does

(Continued on page 178)

(Continued from page 177)

Ronny Willow push me so much?" And her mother said, "Because he likes you!"

Another day, after I had pushed Carol off the sidewalk again, she went home mad. She asked her Grandmother what to do about it and her advice was, "You don't *have* to walk home with that mean Ronny dude!" Thus, that ended my first romantic experience, but my hockey career flourished!
Ron Willow

Crime and Punishment — Second grade, Thomas Lowry School, I had my first experience defying authority. During recess, I was running away from some friends while playing tag and I hid over by the bicycle racks. When I came into school, I had three angry teachers waiting for me. I was severely scolded and marched up to the principal's office, scared to death. The principal was busy, so I had to go back to class until she came to the door. I was crying. When she asked me what happened, I pleaded my case by saying, "I didn't do anything." She figured that they reported the wrong person and apologized.

Then I went back to my desk overcome with guilt. What I meant was that I didn't do any damage. Later, that night, I confessed to my mom who assured me I had committed no great crime and just to forget the whole thing. That was my first experience with the law. **Carol Lyons Larson**

Watching film on crime and punishment

CHAPTER · NINE   CLASS BACKWARDS

Sheridan

Music, Music, Music — Playing in band was a big favorite of mine while growing up. My first band experience was at Logan Park when I was about five, playing in the rhythm band. I loved to play the triangle. Sounds silly now, but at the time that was neat stuff for me.

At Sheridan I joined the band during the summer before fourth grade. Mr. Russell Erickson was the director. He started me on clarinet. I really wanted to play the sax, but had to wait for a year before he'd let me switch to it. I then played sax through ninth grade. I don't know how many times we played the first movement of Schubert's "Unfinished Symphony" but we played and enjoyed it a lot. We also played Sousa marches and a lot of other music. "The Waltz of the Flowers" by Tchaikovsky was another big hit. We especially had fun when we had substitute teachers for band directors. That was when we'd trade and play each others' instruments, with devastating results for the music. I ended up pitying the substitute teachers.   **Louie Paff**

CLASS BACKWARDS — CHAPTER NINE

Lunchtime — We all walked to school so we walked home at lunch time as well. Sometimes someone would have to eat at school because no one was home. Sheridan did not have a lunch room for the grade-schoolers. So they would sit and eat at their desk and promise to be good until they could go outside and play.

For those of us who went home for lunch, we had an hour or more off. We would try to hurry to get back in time to play some game with the others before class like Captain May I? Other games were Stairs, Sliding, Cut the Pie, marbles, softball, tag, Pump-Pump-Pull-away, Red Rover, jump rope, jacks, hopscotch, Stretch, golf-ball bouncing, hop scotch, four-five-six, a-larry… what in the world a-larry was or meant I don't think anyone knew. Having marbles, golf balls, jacks meant my teacher usually got them and put them in her desk. Most of the time we did not get them back. But it was embarrassing when the bag of marbles rolled all over the floor.

There were gender lines for the games and in most cases we did not cross them: Jump rope, jacks, golf ball, and hop scotch usually meant girls; marbles, stretch with a jackknife, were more for boys. The concept of teams for softball did not exist on the playground. All others were whoever showed up or were recruited. Everyone moved through the batting, pitching, catching and fielding part of the game.
Rod Nelson

CHAPTER NINE — CLASS BACKWARDS

Bonding — I attended Sheridan from Kindergarten through 9th grade. Being with so many of the same group of people for so long allowed a great deal of bonding as a group. I still know eight of the people I went through kindergarten with. It allowed us to have a relationship that is really great, a sense of place in this world. **Louie Paff**

A 6th Grade Class To Remember — When we arrived at Sheridan to start the much anticipated 6th grade and being the oldest kids in the world finally, I found that our teacher Mrs. Dahlby was absent. Those of us assigned to her room considered ourselves very lucky for she was the best, the nicest, the one we wanted. Being in 6th grade at Sheridan was to be the oldest kids because we rarely, if ever, saw the 7th through 9th graders in the other part or half of the building. Anyway we arrived to be greeted by a substitute to start our year off. We must have had the right combination of kids in the class because it wasn't many days before we began to feel our oats or test our independence or cleverness.

For whatever reason little nuisance things occurred. Notes were passed. Seats were changed. Giggles and whispering began. Some even dared to make a face behind the sub's back. Our best behavior was absent. Not by all, but enough of us. The sub stayed a few days and then did not return. The next sub arrived and the routines began again. Some new ideas popped up. Pencils dropped on a signal. A mass cough at a certain time. All followed by more giggles and scolding. Once

(Continued on page 182)

Members of that infamous kindergarten class. Left to right: Barbara Thayer, Tom Forenkahm, Wayne Yunker, Judy McClure, Lou Paff, Carolyn Jodie, Rodney Nelson

We have to wonder who was on whom

(Continued from page 181)

again after several days or weeks, she also did not return. The third arrived with a stern warning from our Principal Caroline Barron to be respectful or our parents would be called.
The sub lasted a very short time as well and we were well on our way. One more came and left and our antics had become well honed. We must have learned something along the way, but the sporadic interruptions some of us caused wore them out.

Until Miss Bachlor arrived. Tall, slender, stern, and old as usual. Our plans were set, our routines carried out, but she came back, and she came back after a few weeks as well, and then she refused to leave. We were worn out, exhausted, and we had had plenty of time with her to realize that we were beginning to like her or warm up to her. The antics all stopped by some behind the scenes agreement with each other. We had one wonderful remaining sixth grade year with lots of sadness in having to leave our wonderful amazing teacher.

Rod Nelson

Miss Bachlor—the patient, the revered

CHAPTER · NINE
CLASS BACKWARDS

Pierce, Webster, and Prescott

The Arctic Trek — I especially have a vivid memory of walking to school in the winter.

Imagine being 6 years old and having to walk six city blocks to school. To get there, you had to cross two busy streets- Monroe and Central. OK. I had my sister with me, but still… We were bundled up with snow suits that covered nearly all of our faces. Off we would go, climbing snow banks that must've been ten feet high. That's how they looked to us, anyway. Up and down we would go over those snow banks. Our regular path was six blocks to school, six blocks back home for lunch, six blocks back to school and then home again. No parents walked with us. If it was 20 below zero, we would bring a lunch and eat it at our desk. **Jean Midthun Olsen**

Pierce School of the '40s & '50s

New Friends — Went to Pierce School up to sixth grade. During that period, I remember the streetcar passing down Central Avenue. Also remember my fifth grade teacher, Ms. Spaulding, always making me do art projects. The best I could do was stick figures. Met Ed Zentzis and Bob Peters at Pierce. I remember Ed Zentzis lived in a Quonset hut near the N.E. Athletic Field. **Ray Miller.**

Webster as we saw it.

Margaret Kranz with Sturdy and Sparkle

Happy To Be Here — I started third and fourth grade at Webster Grade School and made many friends. Also, I learned English even better, so that no one would make fun of me.

In about two years, with everyone pitching in, my parents bought their own home on 22nd and Monroe. They were so proud of it and what an accomplishment for them. I was too young to attend Edison High School. But I then attended Prescott for my fifth and sixth grade years. It was quite a walk but I didn't mind. I also spent a lot of time at Jackson Park which was only a block away. It was a wonderful neighborhood. **Nadia Lewacko Yantos**

Special Events

Margaret Kranz a Dental Hygienist — Visited the Minneapolis and St. Paul public schools to educate primary school students in the proper method of maintaining good dental health. As Elementary school children, we were easily persuaded. When Miss Kranz brought her puppets Sturdy and Sparkle to class and talked about dental health, she inspired us all to go home and brush our teeth.

I believe Sturdy convinced us we would have sturdy, healthy bodies if we brushed daily, and Sparkle told us we would light up a room when we smiled with our white teeth.
Carol Lyons Larson

Where Was PETA When You Needed Them? — Sturdy and Sparkle, puppets whose purpose was to get us to brush our teeth etc. would come to visit us in grade school occasionally. In sixth grade, Sturdy and Sparkle brought us two rats. Both got the same food, but one got milk (I think it was a dairy conspiracy) and the other Pepsi to drink. The one who got milk was healthy and robust and the other poor guy was skinny and had bad teeth. We didn't have PETA then (People for the Ethical Treatment of Animals). **Dick Myslajek**

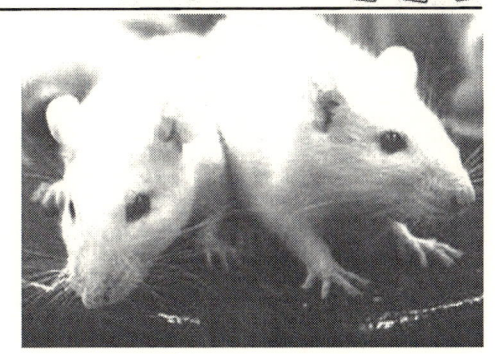

The Circus — A memorable highlight of elementary school was the arrival of the Shrine Circus set up at the Minneapolis Auditorium. We could go if we went with some adult and if we had purchased tickets ahead of time. Thomas Lowry School let us out early, and my mom met us on the corner. We ran to the streetcar to get a good seat near the conductor. Along the way we ate our homemade ham salad sandwiches, anticipating the fun afternoon which it always was. The only disappointment was that I was never permitted to buy one of the live chameleons which vendors sold at the circus.
Mary Kranak Cheleen

Fun Fests and Fundraisers —
Sixth grade, I had my first male teacher, Mr. Acko. He was rather unorthodox in teaching style, but we learned a lot from him. Not satisfied with the itinerant music teacher's biweekly appearance, he taught us to sing various songs, often in French, like "Frere Jacques" and "Angels We Have Heard On High." Every year, Pillsbury had a Fun Fest as a fund raiser. All of the classrooms were transformed by the PTA into event centers, usually various games and contests. The whole neighborhood was invited. We got a couple of tickets free and bought additional tickets for a nickel apiece and toured the rooms and games of our choice.

Bob Buntrock

Paper Sales —
Remember them? At Sheridan, they happened a few times a year. I recall mainly the ones in the fall. Each classroom was pitted against the others to see who could collect the most papers. I don't recall if we won a prize, but it was a great way to instill recycling in us, get a lot of exercise, and teach us unforgettable lessons in competition and team building.

You needed a few friends, a wagon, some binder twine, and enthusiasm. One person would go up to a house and ring the doorbell or knock on the door. If someone answered, we asked if they had any newspapers they could give us. Most times we would receive a small stack, but sometimes we hit the jackpot –

(Continued on page 187)

(Continued from page 186)

several piles!! We would load them on the wagon and when it was full, if we were lucky, one of the fathers would load them in his car and drive to the school, find the correct place for our offering, and then help us unload them. Signs were attached to the outside walls of the school with each room number and teacher's name so we knew where to pile our papers. We watched each room's pile of papers to see who had the most, sometimes with envy. After the "judging" a big truck would park on the street and load up the huge collection. Sometimes we would load them directly into the truck –a different pile for each classroom. Another job well done, and then back to class and learning. But, wasn't it fun? **Carolyn Jodie Hagford**

An Extra Bonus — Sometimes the boys would disappear into the back of the truck or an area hidden behind the piles to look at found comic books. These were hidden to pick up later. And of course the "girlie" magazines certainly took our minds off of loading trucks or working the pile. **Rod Nelson**

Paper Sale Fundraiser — We had annual or semi-annual paper drives. Each room had a designated area on the curb and when the semi came later in the day, each pile was weighed and recorded. The room with the most poundage won some sort of award. If the entire school raised enough money, the whole school was treated to an afternoon of movies: cartoons, and comedies. **Bob Buntrock**

Teachers' Strike — Early in 1948, while we were in second grade, probably right at the start of the second semester, the Minneapolis school teachers went on strike. I was torn. Part of me welcomed the extra "vacation" but the other part of me wanted to go back to school as usual. Possibly because I missed close to half of first grade on and off due to a number of illnesses, I was just hitting my stride and enjoying the school experience. As I recall, the strike lasted into March with a couple of false starts on our return. I do remember one morning walking with my mother up to Pillsbury school on a sunny, cold winter day because we had heard there was the possibility that school would resume. It didn't and we had to wait a few days more.
Bob Buntrock

How About A Pillsbury School Wide Picnic — We had a special casserole lunch day that our mothers prepared and served. Most memorable was the school picnic at Windom Park where we had three legged races, regular races, ball throws etc. About 450 kids spread out on blankets all over the park. Thinking about it now, there must have been a lot fewer mothers then because most of us had brothers or sisters at the school with us.   **Gordie Solz**

Practice Makes Perfect — At Sheridan we would practice marching on the field a couple of times for the parade down Nicollet. We never won any trophies as far as I remember. Some of us didn't participate in the games being held 'cause we just kept our shoes on and walked down the center of the creek from the Falls to the river. Nobody missed us. We really felt special and unique because we conquered the distance and the creek. There was a price, however. Drenched and missing our streetcar home with the others, we had to take the streetcar by ourselves. At the big picnic new bikes had been set aside for a special school drawing. Once schools were drawn as a bike winner, someone's ticket from that school would be drawn. It was also a way to get us all together for the streetcar rides home. Who wouldn't want to win a bike? Did you win one?
Rod Nelson

Safety Patrol Parade and Picnic — Sixth Graders throughout the city could be crossing guards. You got out five minutes early for lunch and were allowed back five minutes late. "Off duty" was the call from corner to corner to say we could leave and go back to school. The reward was marching in a parade downtown with guards from all over the city in June plus a T-shirt and a free drink ticket at the annual big picnic for patrols at Minnehaha Park.
Bob Buntrock

Sheridan on Parade

Minnehaha Falls

Digging Deeper—School Memories K-6

Gordie Solz — Recalling a Few More Things at Pillsbury

Kindergarten: was a memorable year for me. I never used the bathrooms at school, but went home and came back when finished. I must have been sneaky because I was never caught (except my mother who kept telling me not to do that.) My big accomplishment was making a cutting board in the shape of a pig. I think it is still at my parents' house.

1st Grade: Miss Murphy was a great reading teacher. We read almost every day in groups according to how adept you were. I was pretty good, but really lousy at the easel with the paints.

2nd Grade: We were with 3rd graders. Miss McLaughlin was probably the best teacher we ever had. She would find out what you we were the best at and give you something that was more advanced. I was a little gifted in math so she gave me a 5th grade math book to use. My claim to fame that year was that we made our mothers a sprinkling bottle for ironing clothes.

CHAPTER NINE CLASS BACKWARDS

3rd Grade: Mrs. Mee. Everyday we listened at 11:00 am to Tommy Bartlett's "Welcome Travelers" at some Chicago railroad station on the radio. The most exciting thing that year was that she locked Gordy Loye in the closet and went home and left him there. Luckily, the janitor heard him and let him out. It was a Friday so it would have been a helluva weekend.

4th Grade: We had 12 or 13 different teachers. I was in love with Miss Johnston, our first, and was devestated when her husband was transferred by the Air Force to Colorado. A few of the many to follow were really impressed by our knowledge of the order of the Presidents. I don't know if any of them ever figured out we knew the street names. It took Mrs. Olsen, our last one, only 15 minutes to restore sanity and without the principal's help.

5th Grade: We were with 6th graders. We figured we got rooked because we didn't have an afternoon recess but Mrs. Stickel's - the other fifth grade - still got it.

6th Grade: Mr. Acko really brought us up to date with a few of his lectures. He went ballistic one day and stated "Boys and girls, you are developing into men and women. You girls are developing breasts and the boys are developing. . ." (He never did finish). He also played the accordion for us. That was at the top of the list.

Carolyn Hagford-A Quick Stroll - Sheridan Elementary

Kindergarten: Our room was a large room at the end of the hall with big windows that let in the sun. It shone on our easels as we painted gigantic wonderful pictures with tempera paints. My parents were so proud of every one I brought home. Every Monday, someone was chosen to carry the American flag and lead the rest of the class in our march around the room. That was the day we brought our pennies to school for the Red Cross and we dropped them into a glass jar as we passed by.

There was a large box in the room on legs that kept it about 18 inches off the floor. It was filled with sand and I loved playing in it. Once, I slipped my hand in the box to run my fingers through the sand - so nice. But Miss Woodward saw me, came over and slapped my hand, telling me in a stern voice that I was not allowed to touch the sand because it was the boy's day to play in the sandbox. Oops.

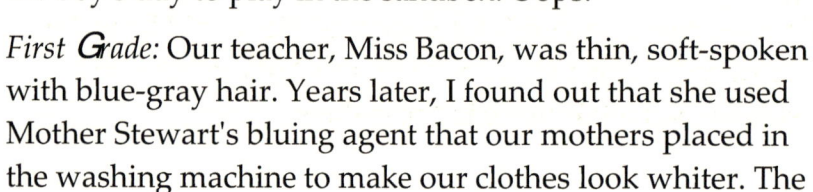

First Grade: Our teacher, Miss Bacon, was thin, soft-spoken with blue-gray hair. Years later, I found out that she used Mother Stewart's bluing agent that our mothers placed in the washing machine to make our clothes look whiter. The one thing I remember about her was that every day as we went out for recess she told us we should always go out and come back 'like little butterflies.' In other words, be quiet children.

Second Grade: Miss Latendress(were none of them married?) was a heavier woman with big bosoms and she must have had some skin condition. She was constantly scratching her neck behind her ear in a fast, manic mode. I guess it wasn't contagious because none of us 'caught' anything.

Third Grade: Miss Estes always wore pretty dresses. She was a nice teacher because she never scared me. I always did my work, so that may have been the reason.

I can't recall which grade, but I remember singing lessons. Our instructor, from outside of Sheridan, taught us how to read music and follow her directing so that we could sing fun songs. Occasionally, we had mini-tests and those that sang the best were told to sit in the back seats of each row. This way, the others with lesser capabilities could hear the "good ones." I was in the back seat most of the time, so I must have had a fair voice in those days.

Louie Paff – Elementary School Inspired My Life - Sheridan

One of the memorable things about kindergarten was the day they drew shadow drawings of our heads using the cloak room with the lights out and a bright bulb (projector?) to trace our silhouette on paper. Anyone still have it?

In our elementary classrooms we always sat in straight rows. There was none of the creative seating that one sees in school these days. The desks were the old style with wrought iron frames. Wood was used for the desktop, and the back, and the seat which folded up. But that doesn't mean our teachers weren't creative.

Second Grade: The school district brought in a music teacher from the MacPhail school of music to teach us to read music. It was wonderful that they did that! I picked up reading music quickly from her and was elated with my new skill. I also learned solfeggio from her (do re mi fa sol la ti do plus the names for the half steps). We could join the band in fourth grade. So I played clarinet, then sax. Having the music reading skill was a great band ad-

(Continued on page 195)

CHAPTER NINE — CLASS BACKWARDS

(Continued from page 194)

vantage. I played in band from fourth grade on through part of college and then became a music major. I have been involved in music all my life and am so thankful for that lady from MacPhail.

Third Grade: I remember the day in that we were first introduced to cursive handwriting. Our teacher printed "like" on the blackboard (the boards were truly black back then), and then she wrote "like" in cursive right over the printed "like". It was a great illustration! Then we did the same thing followed by a few more words. I looked at my cursive; it was horrible. I looked at my classmate's paper, her desk was right across the aisle, and her cursive was gorgeous. I knew right then that life isn't fair and I was destined to a life of terrible writing. It has truly been borne out. It didn't matter how much I practiced. It never improved. I was so happy when I was able to get a laptop computer to take notes on, and I've been able to read what I've written ever since.

Fourth Grade: Our teacher talked to us many times about her adventures while living in what was then called Malaya. She talked about the natives hunting in the jungle with poison dart blowguns. It all seemed exotic and fascinating to me, enough so that I

(Continued on page 196)

(Continued from page 195)

wanted a similar experience when I when I grew up. So after college graduation I joined the Peace Corps and loved for two years in Liberia with its tropical rain forests.

Sixth Grade: We were terrors. We went through five teachers that year before getting a teacher who didn't need to "tough it out with us." The first five teachers gave up on us as being uncontrollable. Not all of us were "bad," but a goodly portion of the class was terribly troublesome.

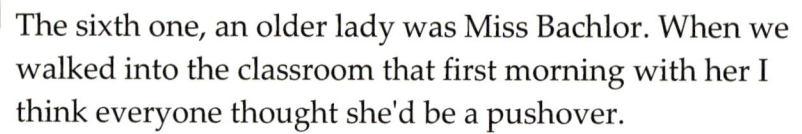

Five down

The sixth one, an older lady was Miss Bachlor. When we walked into the classroom that first morning with her I think everyone thought she'd be a pushover.

We were so wrong. She sat at her desk silently until the bell rang, and then started talking softly. The students were yelling and having a good old time. But gradually the class noticed that the students nearest her desk had become quiet and were really listening to what she was saying. So in a short period of time the whole class became quiet because she was saying such interesting things. She never raised her voice ever, and we students enjoyed the rest of the school year immensely.

And the intrepid Mrs. Bachlor

I became a teacher and taught for 46 years before retiring. I've always wondered what she said that first day because she was magic with students. If I could remember clearly how she did it I would have incorporated part of it into my teaching.

CHAPTER TEN:

GETTIN' AROUND

In the city, we relied on streetcars to get us around, but we did a lot of far-distance walking too. Many of us will never forget the chug-a-chug rhythm of the streetcar and the neighborly relationships it seemed to foster.

Train travel was in its glory. Our generation would remember the train whistle in the night before the steam locomotives were replaced by diesel locomotives. Many of us lived within or right by trains tracks or routes. The layout of early Northeast Minneapolis led to more train switchyards and crossings that seemed to reach into all neighborhoods. It was nearly impossible to travel any distance without going over or under a train bridge. Some of us traveled via the trains, but most of us enjoyed them somewhat from a distance or hearing them rush by from the safety of our houses. A few traveled by plane.

Gasoline and rubber had been rationed during the war, but afterwards, car trips became affordable. New pumps at gas stations made it possible for drivers to ask for dollar amounts. By the early '50s, travel in the family car became popular. Trailer parks and campgrounds offered alternatives to motels.

The end of a busy day of shopping or work. Courtesy Minnesota Historical Society

Powers Department Store is to the right and Boutell's Furniture to the left. Courtesy Minnesota Historical Society

Streetcars

Nice, Noisy, and Easy — For the most part, our moms didn't drive the family car just for daily transportation around the city. What was more common was to use the streetcars to go downtown to see a movie or to shop. Streetcars ran on electricity drawn from overhead wires with steel upon steel clattering repeatedly on the tracks.

At least once a week, my mom walked one-half mile and took a streetcar from 28th and Johnson to downtown Minneapolis. When she brought me with her, she made me feel like a treasured companion. I used to watch her, this mother of mine, strike up a conversation with someone seated near her and soften the most sour, reserved person into a relatively pleasant acquaintance. People she met regularly along the way and working downtown became her friends. Even the female detective from Powers Department store met her for pie in the afternoon.

 I learned how to shop for bargains, sure, but she crystallized a way for me to counteract loneliness. She had found a niche for herself, as if it were her workplace.   **Carol Lyons Larson**

Noise in the Night — Occasionally, we would stay over the weekend at grandma's house. The first night's sleep was broken up about every half hour. A street car would go by (about 20 feet from the house) and shake, rattle and roll. It would go to the end of the line on Grand Street and Lowry and come back down and do the same thing all over again- all night long ! The second night you never heard them. I think we got used to them or we were too whipped to hear them. But at 1:00 AM we had the extra attraction of the Spring Inn and M&M bars closing and a couple hundred people heading for home. Most of them walked because they lived in the neighborhood, and they usually didn't walk too straight and a lot of them sang- again, not too straight!
Gordie Solz

Streetcar at 27th and Washington
Courtesy Minnesota Historical Society

Bus Rides — My mother took the bus downtown to go shopping every week, but she usually didn't take the kids along. She would meet a friend and have lunch. I think it was one of the highlights of her week. **Norm Solberg**

A Great Shopping Area — East Hennepin brought many folks together especially on Friday night: J.C. Penney, Ward's, Sears, Nelson Paints, Ben Franklin, Woolworth's, Eklund's Men's Clothing Store, and a drug store, plus a few smaller shops and a bank. There was also a theater, on Fourth Street called "The Princess Theater." The shopping district was about two blocks long on East Hennepin from University to Fifth on both sides of the street.

My mom would get on the streetcar weekly which was a block away and go downtown. Of course, she would take me. If I was good she would buy me candy, like chocolate-covered peanuts. When I got home, I was exhausted from keeping up with my mom. **Jean Torgerson Strong**

Note the Eklund sign on the left.

The Electric Stagecoach — It was a familiar sight to see a yellow streetcar wait on the tracks while passengers climbed aboard. Fast and noisy, it had a wire mesh cowcatcher drooping front, as it came to a halt. The doors would clatter open as we scampered up the steps, dropped a dime in the box, and ran for a seat by an open window.

The conductor's hand would touch the accelerator, and the electric motors whirred into life. The clacking sound of wheel on rail picked up the rhythm as we gained speed. Near the next corner, the screeching protest of steel against steel pierced our ears as we braked for a stop.

(Continued on page 201)

Chapter Ten

Class Backwards

(Continued from page 200)

As kids, Red Lyons and I would run for a seat with an open window and take aim at the trees with our shiny cap pistols as we would begin a long, slow climb. We would turn around and pick at the wicker back, and then settle back in our seat, place our feet on the metal ledge, and lean our heads outside the window. Edging past the crest of the hill, the streetcar would race down the other side. The wind blew our shirt sleeves and splashed the hair from our eyes. Like a latter-day stagecoach, the streetcar swayed and pitched down its violent course.

What kept it on the tracks? I wondered. It was a ride for cowboys and kids, true connoisseurs of adventure and the wild, wild West.

From a story written by Dana Watten, class of '55.

Harmless Fun — The streetcar stopped at the corner of 33rd Avenue and Johnson Street NE. to let the last passengers off the car. When it turned around and started up again, the boys in our neighborhood would take the streetcar downtown to see a movie, go to Woolworth's or Kresge's, and top the day off at Bridgeman's with a banana split or a triple treat.

We were outside most of the day with very little supervision but once the curfew sounded its horn at 9:30 at night, we were off the streets and in our homes. We did not want to be

(Continued on page 202)

(Continued from page 201)

brought home by the police. Whatever happened to that concept?

It was a good time and place to grow up.
Dodd Knutsen (Class of '59)

Playing Pranks — We lived 3½ blocks from the Bryant/Johnson carline. Some kids were always playing pranks. Placing coins on the tracks before a car came was a harmless stunt. It was usually a penny because that's all they could afford. I tried a few when visiting down the street. The other thing they tried (but was riskier) was to put a roll of cap gun caps on the track. The bang was pretty potent but that attracted more attention including the neighbors who were as sore as the motormen were. **Bob Buntrock**

Smashing Fun — One of the enjoyments at my grandparents' house on Monroe was the street cars. We put different things on the tracks for them to run over and squish (or smash). A piece of glass became very sharp sand, but the favorite was a penny. It took a few trips to make it big enough and flat enough to show off. **Gordie Solz**

My Dancing Career — I remember taking the streetcar on Saturday mornings to my dancing lessons downtown at MacPhail School of Music—all by myself. I must have been 7 or 8. I was in second grade at that time. Isn't it odd that my folks didn't even worry about me going alone, and I wasn't afraid either? I knew the way. And then the buses took the place of the streetcars as I continued my dancing career at MacPhail, maybe until 8th grade. And now you know why they call me the Cyd Charisse of Northeast Minneapolis.
Bev Warren

MacPhail School of Music

Streetcar stuck in the snow

Icy Souvenirs — I remember riding the streetcar in Minneapolis. We'd use it to go downtown when I was little. It ran right down Johnson Street and ran on Hennepin Avenue. Later when I started to drive, the streetcars were gone but the tracks were still there, and during the winter they caused a car to swerve around when it was icy. **Norm Solberg**

Woolworths post card's

The End of a Line — We lived near the end-of-the-line of the Bryant Johnson streetcar line which was at 33rd and Johnson. Along the tracks were wooden pavers. The streetcars ran on electricity provided by overhead wires and on steel tracks.

In the late '40s and early '50s my mother would give me a dollar and along with my neighborhood friends Jim Terry, Dale Halverson and Dodd Knutson, we would walk the three blocks to catch the streetcar to go downtown. We usually made a day of it. It was a ten cent token each way, a movie was 12 cents, a hot dog and a coke at Woolworths or Kresges was about 30 cents and I would have money left over to buy something.

Once we packed a lunch and rode the Bryant - Johnson to the other end of the line somewhere in South Minneapolis and back. Of course, I felt like I was going out of town.

In the '50s, local crooks with the help of big companies took the streetcars away so they could replace them with buses. I'm still burned by it!   **Dick Myslajek**

*Out with the streetcars
Here come the buses*

Scrap — When they took the streetcars off line, they ripped up a lot of the tracks and sold them for scrap and they also took the poles holding the electric lines overhead and did the same.

A few people we knew were sent to jail for doing this and not reporting it. When they took the poles off the Central Bridge they left holes in the walkway and a young kid went through one of the holes and down to the tracks below. **Gordie Solz**

Ripping up the streetcar rails

Train Travel

The Other Side of The Tracks — Railroad tracks and trains were part of lower N.E. Getting near them was always a somewhat scary experience when you are 6-9 years old. We moved into our house on 2nd Street and 15th. Trains and tracks became part of life. We had a coal burner for heating. Dad would send me with my wagon down Broadway to the train tracks to pick up the coal that fell off the cars. This was not an enjoyable way to spend my time as a 7-8 year old and luckily, it lasted only a few weeks. Guess, I never found enough or Mother stepped in. I also walked up to the Nut House (although I only knew it as the Northeast Neighborhood House) further north on 2nd Street. We had to cross massive tracks and many times, we waited for a train by the mill's si-

A train up close

(Continued on page 206)

(Continued from page 205)

los. At another site, Bottineau Park, we went to the chain link fence protecting us and watched the freight train, while we sometimes waved at the passengers. But the thing about the trains was that at an early age, I found when up close to the massive engines — they scared the hell out of me. I was not sure what their capabilities were and if I could be pulled into those huge wheels. The noise was also deafeningly scary. It made no difference whether it was still or moving slowly. Even walking across so many tracks had its own terror, wondering when and if. . . Stories did abound of kids jumping and riding the trains. Then of course, you would hear of some boy who lost an arm or leg while playing on or near them. When I was more pushing teen years and I had to wait for a stopped or slow moving train, I would challenge myself to visualize if I could crawl under a car before the train moved. Never tried it. Finally, I did jump trains as a young adult. **Rod Nelson**

Down in the Valley — I did spend a lot of time at Grandparents' on Spring and Monroe (Two blocks from the yard) and could run across about 10 sets of tracks. On Sundays when we finished dinner we would then squeeze into our uncle's '35 Ford coupe with a rumble seat and he would haul us down to the Princess Theater on 4th Street just off East Hennepin.

Someone had best tell the streetcar motorman that is a train coming through the mill

The Princess Theater

CHAPTER TEN   CLASS BACKWARDS

Before we left, we were instructed by either grandpa or grandma that we were to go over the bridge on 5th Street and not to go across the tracks on the way home. Well, after a couple of comedies and a double feature along with a nickel pop and a nickel popcorn we exited and headed for the 5th st bridge. There was a slight detour on the way- to the tracks. We lined up side by side, looked both ways, then, scared as hell, ran across the tracks and up to the far side of the 5th Street bridge and climbed up the side to the street. **Gordie Solz**

Rare Sighting — One day in Mr. Kemp's 7th grade Common Learnings class just before the holidays, at a quiet moment, I turned around in my window seat and spotted a huge 4-8-8-4 Mallet steam engine chugging down the Northern Pacific tracks past the football field. It was pulling at least 100 loaded iron ore cars. We had never seen this combination on the NP and assumed that the Lakes had iced in early so the mines decided to get one more shipment out by rail. Very impressive! **Bob Buntrock**

Engine 4012 above is one of a very few articulate steam engines built. Designed to haul heavy loads and still be able to maneuver around the bends in the roads. This engine has four leading wheels, 8 driving wheels, followed by 8 more driving wheels and 4 following wheels giving it the designation of 4-8-8-4.

207

Warnings — I was a Hill kid so the closest I got to the tracks was when at Edison. Of course, anywhere you went in town, car, bus, street car, you were within sight of tracks and viaducts. My Dad had worked on the railroad as a teenager (spike mauler) and was interested in trains which he passed on to me. I was cautioned not to be anywhere near any train tracks especially when a train was approaching.
Bob Buntrock

Sad Story — While Fred Brandt and I were looking for iron slugs for our sling shots, Fred went between the couplings and reached the track when the train moved. The train ran over his arm. I ran to stop the train. Then I ran and wrapped his arm in a jacket. Bad experience. **Ray Miller**

From the Bridges —-I lived six blocks north of East Hennepin, and walked over the railroad bridges on University Avenue and Fourth Street innumerable times. Until I was a teenager I loved going to those bridges to see the steam trains rumble below me throwing up clouds of steam and smoke on either side of the bridge.

It was fun for awhile to pick up pebbles and drop them on the trains passing below.

(Continued on page 209)

(Continued from page 208)

My friends and I talked about hopping on a slow moving train but never did it because of not knowing where we'd end up if a train sped up and worrying about falling under the wheels. It was exciting to contemplate.

I was totally used to the sight, sounds, and smoke of trains, and never gave much thought to the idea that I was living in a place that was unusual because of all the trains.
Louie Paff

Viaducts — I had to walk under the viaduct to get to my new home from school, which was Sheridan. Viaducts were new to me and very scary. So when I should have walked under them I would run as fast as I could. It was dark and dirty under there. There were several viaducts in NE. Often you could really be brave and run under them when a train was passing over.   **Jean Torgerson Strong**

Run, Don't Walk! — Viaducts were in my life only when I attended Edison. If I had to stay after school in the winter, it was scary, scary, scary to walk through the darkness alone. Anyone could be hiding behind those thick pillars. I went as fast as I could. Usually running until I reached the other side – alive!   **Carolyn Hagford**

My Big Adventure — One summer I experienced a train ride from Thief River Falls to Minneapolis coming into the Milwaukee Depot. My Grandma put me on the train with a big lunch and I think I ate all the way to Minneapolis. It was a night train and I know I irritated some folks on the train especially when I dragged out the chips. I think back on it and have to laugh. My mom met me in the morning when I got off. I never slept a wink. **Jean Torgerson Strong**

Milwaukee Depot

Trains — If there was one thing I could bring back and relive, it would be train travel – specifically the way it was done in the prime time of train travel back in the '40s and '50s – more specifically on a Pullman car. In the late '40s my mother and I took the train to North Carolina where my dad was temporarily working. The trip started at the Great Northern Depot – unfortunately since razed – a massive building on Hennepin Avenue just south of the Mississippi River where trains would be coming and going on a regular schedule. The depot was a monument to train travel. On the Pullman car the porter would come and convert your seating area into bunk beds with curtains for privacy . The service was impeccable and the dining car was special – white linen, and food prepared by chefs on the train. It was special and there is nothing like it today. **Dick Myslajek**

Pullman Ad between '42 & '46

210

Great Northern Depot
Note the streetcar safety island in the foreground and the Grain Belt Beer sign in the background across the river.
July 1951

Sentimental Journey — On special occasions, my mother would take me on the train to visit my grandparents in Sandstone for a few days. At the Great Northern Depot, her anticipation was contagious, amplified by echoing voices of railroad employees announcing the arrivals and departures of trains. One of our rituals was to stop and gaze at the huge mural of the Blackfoot and Kootenai Indian powwows, hanging on one of the walls. After paying our respects to the painting, my mom would purchase our tickets as I would peek out a dingy window to the tracks below. With wonderment, I would realize that I was soon to board one of those trains. We were characters in a high drama. The trip took four hours. Scenes of the countryside entertained us as did a porter going up and down the aisle selling sandwiches. They were dry and thinly spread but we savored them.
Carol Lyons Larson

Hobos – A Culture So Near — We would venture up to 37th Avenue and walk along the railroad tracks. After the War, there would be hobos camped along the tracks. I can still recall the man in the bushy white beard who was cooking something over an open fire. He seemed old at the time but I'm not so sure of that anymore. It seemed like quite an adventure to be riding the rails traveling the country although we were oblivious to the hardships these poor people faced. **Dodd Knutsen**

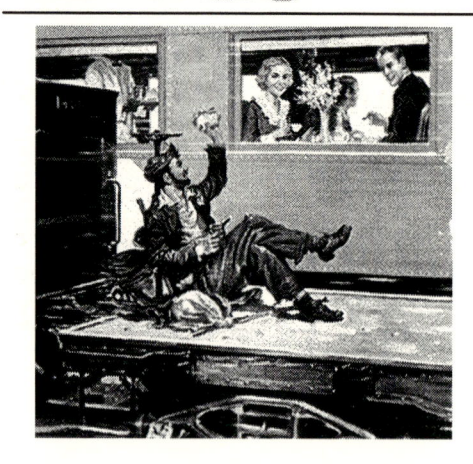

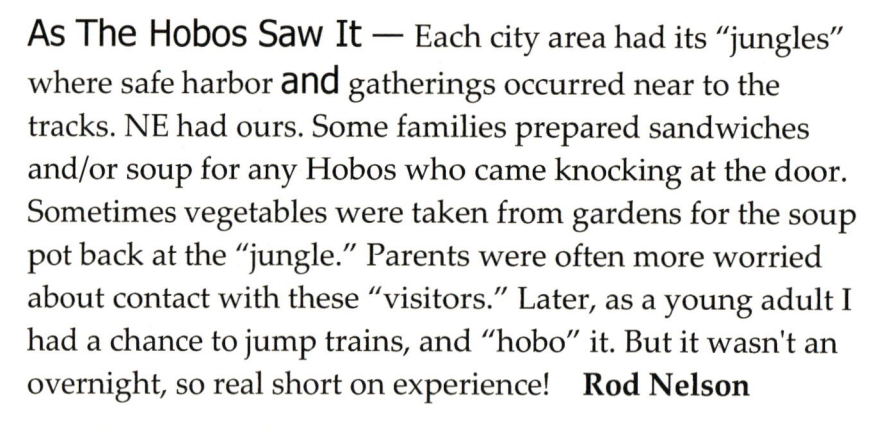

As The Hobos Saw It — Each city area had its "jungles" where safe harbor **and** gatherings occurred near to the tracks. NE had ours. Some families prepared sandwiches and/or soup for any Hobos who came knocking at the door. Sometimes vegetables were taken from gardens for the soup pot back at the "jungle." Parents were often more worried about contact with these "visitors." Later, as a young adult I had a chance to jump trains, and "hobo" it. But it wasn't an overnight, so real short on experience! **Rod Nelson**

Trips Outside the City

Visiting Other States and Parks — In the early '50s, our family started taking trips. They almost always involved my aunt, uncle, and two cousins.. Two week trips (corresponding to vacation days) were set up for the mid July period. In consecutive years we went to the Black Hills, New York-Washington, D.C, the Ozarks via Nashville, and Winnipeg. The destinations were different, but the planning and readying for the trips was all the same and fell totally on Mother. Accommodations were always tenting in the State Parks or available campgrounds even just outside New York City and right in heart of Washington, D.C. I didn't realize that we were privileged to be able to see America in a less busy, less populated time and free of a lot of the spoils of over use.

Mother planned menus, decided who would wear what

Carolyn Jody & family at Mount Rushmore

(Continued on page 213)

(Continued from page 212)

when, laid all things out, and packed the suitcases. The main food items (to be cooked on a Coleman stove) were purchased and packed with all the camping gear. On the day of departure a trailer was loaded with all the gear and the trunk was packed as well. We had our books or games we could play in the car, but mostly we preferred to look out the windows at all the sights never seen before. With three kids in the backseat and one up front with Mother and Dad, the family was on its way. Dad drove and mother bought rolls and milk at a small town bakery for a breakfast snack. Lunch times, Dad would catnap after eating peanut butter and jelly sandwiches or again fresh bakery bread and cold cuts. We usually got to play in a town's park for awhile. The same procedures took place on all family trips.

We also had the experience of going as a family to Minnesota State Parks and camping for two weeks. Itasca, Scenic St. Croix, but we returned mostly to Scenic State Park – our favorite. Some years Dad would return to the city and work leaving Mother in charge of us for the next weeks. We swam, fished, and hiked daily. I saw sunrises, full moons, and an eclipse from a fire tower. We picked blueberries, raspberries if in season, and had our chores washing dishes and putting things away after the meals. We got the ice which was stored in sawdust in the upper level of a camp building. Gathering firewood, and playing with kids from other families we would see, year after year kept us busy as well. **Rod Nelson**

Home town bakery

A young and apparently lucky Rod Nelson

Our Car — We had a 1935 Chevrolet Standard two door. There was no trunk, so our luggage went in the back seat alongside me. The trips were always sweltering because my mother couldn't stand a draft on her neck, so we drove in the hot summer sun with all the windows closed in our black car. We did start trips at around 5:30 or 6:00 in the morning to avoid the heat, but returning was often later in the day. I remember the 6 cylinder motor really humming at 50 mph, and that's about the fastest we drove. Flat tires on the trip were common — those rayon cords weren't very strong. I loved the vacations because I got to play on the farms that we always stayed at. Family reunions were always on farms and were always great fun! **Louie Paff**

Taking the Bus to Camp — One summer my sister and I went to camp for a week. We took a bus to the lake, slept in cabins, and ate in a mess hall. And then there were the outhouses that we had to use even at night. The counselors tried to teach us how to swim, took us on nature walks, and how to make plaster *apres doe* prints.

At night when the counselors thought we were sleeping they would leave the cabin. We, however, were just pretending and then the fun would start. Only I was really sleeping and nobody could wake me up even though they tried every night and the party was in our cabin!! So I slept through the best memories of the trip. **Joanne Rau**

Going to Camp — I guess I was lucky for having so many traveling experiences as a youngster. But like many other kids, I also attended a two-week residence neighborhood house camp. I did this for five plus years as well as squeezing in a week to go to Manypoint Scout Camp.

I must admit as a teenager, I really didn't want to go on the family vacations as much. I loved the summer camps though. I guess I preferred to be with my peers more than away some-where with the family, although the places visited and sights seen were never boring. While in the car, I busied myself with looking out the car windows at all the sights along the way, which to me was, and still is, of the utmost interest.
Rod Nelson

Trips? - I don't remember any trips. In the summer, we would go to the Barry House and a bus would pick us up and we went for 50 cents to the Camden Pool. Some children went to a day camp at Stanley's Place on Turtle Lake. Other than that, we played over at Beltrami Park and at the Barry House.
Ray Miller

What Camp? - I think it was Icogawahn- not sure. But I went there with Birger Kylander, Bob Johnson, John Vandermyde, my cousin Ed Solz, my brother Doug and my cousin Dan Kaedden (plus a few others). I think Lydia Olsen's brother was a counselor. I didn't want to go home until the lights went out the first night.   **Gordie Solz**

215

Northwestern National Bank Weather Ball
Courtesy Minnesota Historical Society

Weather Was Important — In the mid to late '40s right after World War II, we would go to Lake Sarah where my grandparents had a small resort on the lake. At that time, it was about a 2-hour drive from our home in Northeast Minneapolis. Now it would be maybe 45 minutes. In the '40s we had to travel north all the way to the end of Lowry Avenue and then take a couple of highways to get there. Nothing about packing or planning seemed to be an issue but what was an issue was how we could only go when the weather was nice. If it was raining, it affected the picnic, the swimming, fishing and all of the fun we usually had once we arrived. Since there was no phone at the lake, it was understood that if the weather was not good, we wouldn't be there and if the weather was nice, we would arrive as scheduled. Is it not amazing that we seemed to communicate clearly without all the modern technology — in fact without any real means of formal communication after a trip was once scheduled? We had a plan and followed it, I guess.

Now for the fun part of this story. The way we checked the weather was by walking over to Central Avenue and seeing what color was on the weather ball at Northwestern National Bank!

I can still remember the jingle: "Weather Ball blinking white, rainy weather is in sight, Weather Ball red as fire, temperature is going higher. Weather Ball is steady green, then there

(Continued on page 217)

(Continued from page 216)

is no change foreseen." So we watched the Weather Ball and then jumped in the car if it looked good.

Our car was another issue. We'd pack up and leave home and get about 2/3 of the way up Lowry and the car would die. It happened almost every time we went. The dreaded Vapor Lock!!

We would all pile out of the car and sit on the curb until the car cooled down and then sometimes it would start and sometimes it wouldn't – more waiting. Finally – for whatever reason, with all the men in the family hanging over the hood speculating and poking things it would start! We would hop back in and go as fast as possible to try to make it again before Vapor Lock struck again. Who knows what it really was, but for me at about 6-10 years old it meant a miserable trip. All was forgotten once we arrived, however, and we were in for a real fun day or weekend.

Sandy Cederstrom Rorem

Almost Paradise — The family trips I remember most fondly were when we went to our cabin at Coon Lake, about an hour away. It was rustic (no electricity for a while, an outhouse, a pump with iron-tasting water, mostly one big room that we'd partition off with some drapes. The cabin was at the end of the road, so that beyond was just a great big woods. There were millions of frogs, and I guiltily remember

Vapor Lock struck again

(Continued on page 218)

(Continued from page 217)

using them for target practice with my jackknife. Once when we drove up, a goat was wandering around our cabin. The family stayed in the car while my father tried to drive the goat away, running around and around the cabin. I don't know why my father didn't just let the goat stay, but I suppose he was protecting his children from getting butted. There were a number of skunks, garter snakes and other wildlife. Out on the lake there were many painted turtles, which we'd catch in our boat and play with. There were also many bullheads to catch in the lake. They weren't very good eating, but they put up a great fight landing them. It was like paradise for a kid. **Norm Solberg**

Where did we go last summer?

Trips Not Taken — It must've been a requirement that almost every year at the start of each grade school year each student had to stand up and tell about some trip or event from the prior summer. Maybe because we didn't have a car or maybe I just had a boring life, it seemed with few exceptions I didn't have anything I thought worth relating. So while others were excitedly telling their stories I was trying to look invisible, trying to think of a made up story and hoping the teacher wouldn't get to me. Then the few years we did take an interesting trip, the teacher never asked – not that I wanted to stand up and tell anyone anyway.
Dick Myslajek

Fishing Trips — One fishing trip, my friend and I locked my mother and her friend in the outhouse. It had a hook on the outside, probably to keep the door closed in the winter. After we locked the door, a large grasshopper sat on the hook. They were in the smelly outhouse for about twenty minutes. My mother kept calling for me while my friend and I hid behind a tree. I was in deep trouble, but there was no way I was going to go near that grasshopper. **Jean Torgerson Strong**

Planes — In the '50s, air travel started to replace trains. At the end of 6th grade (June of 1952), I got out of two weeks of school, again to go with my mother on a trip to where my dad was working as a professional wrestler – this time in New York City. We took off from what was then Wold Chamberlain Field – a small airport by today's standards, just north of the current airport, with a small building from which you walked onto the tarmac – walking up temporary stairs to board the plane. There were no jets then, but Northwest Airline's flew the Stratocruiser – a large four engine, double deck propeller driven plane - the class of its time. I'm not sure, but I seem to recall about 300 mph at about 32,000 feet? **Dick Myslajek**

Northwest Orient Airlines Stratocruiser · Fastest · Finest

CLASS BACKWARDS

CHAPTER TEN

CHAPTER 11:
THE BEGINNING OF A NEW ERA-THE EARLY '50s

Our stories and pictures have become a collage of our past. When we began to leave our grade schools and eventually enter Edison High School, our paths zigged and zagged in many directions. Not only because we were older but also because the upper-grade limits of our grade schools differed. Some of us spent our seventh, eighth and even ninth grade years at our grade school, becoming the leaders and the oldest students. Others spent those years at Edison, being the youngest students there. All of us had to adjust to a departmentalized schedule of different teachers. No wonder we were confused! It was a period of transition, meeting new people and new challenges, uncertain about our place in this new society. Thanks to our upbringing and a strong community, we were full of wonder and had the courage to sort it out, as we were soon to be exposed to a larger world.

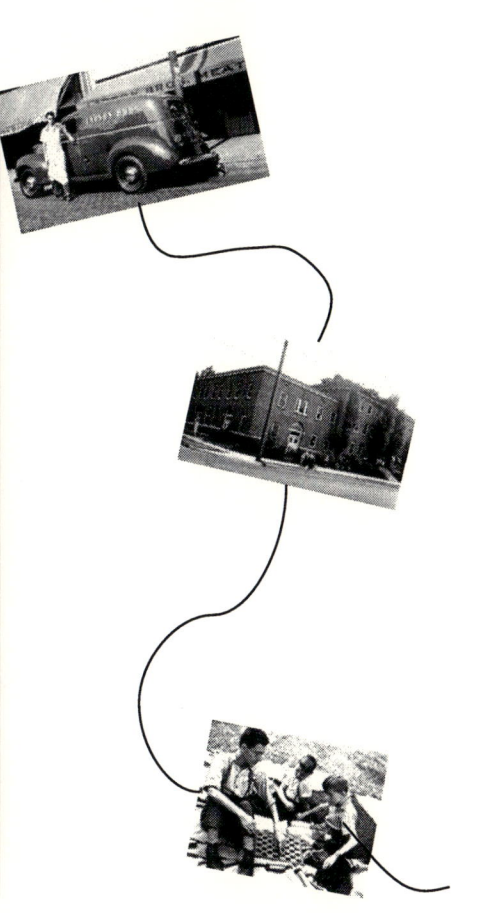

Some Backward Thoughts

Who Were We? — The stories in this book are drawn from our experience during our formative years. Many of the stories could have come from any of the ethnic areas of Northeast Minneapolis. How they all evolved and meshed is a testament to the values given to us by our parents. They created a patchwork known for its cultural heritage made up of second and third-generation Eastern Europeans, Scandinavians, and people from the Mediterranean until we were old enough to move to junior high schools. Junior high school is where we began to learn about the kids from other parts of our beloved Northeast. Our world expanded, for better or for worse. **Bob Peters**

CHAPTER · ELEVEN — CLASS BACKWARDS

Where Did We Came From?

— Seventh graders came from Waite Park School (34th between Ulysses and Garfield), Pillsbury School (22nd and Hayes), Prescott School (Lowry and Taylor), Holland School (17th and Washington), and Edith Cavell School (34th and 35th on Pierce and Fillmore.) Ninth graders came to Edison from Lowry School (29th and Lincoln), Schiller School (27th and California), St. Charles School (27th and Stinson Blvd.), and Holy Cross School (16th and 17th on 4th Street.) Tenth graders came from Sheridan School (Broadway and University), fed by Webster School (Summer and Monroe), Pierce School (Broadway and Fillmore) and Holy Cross School (17th and 4th Street.)

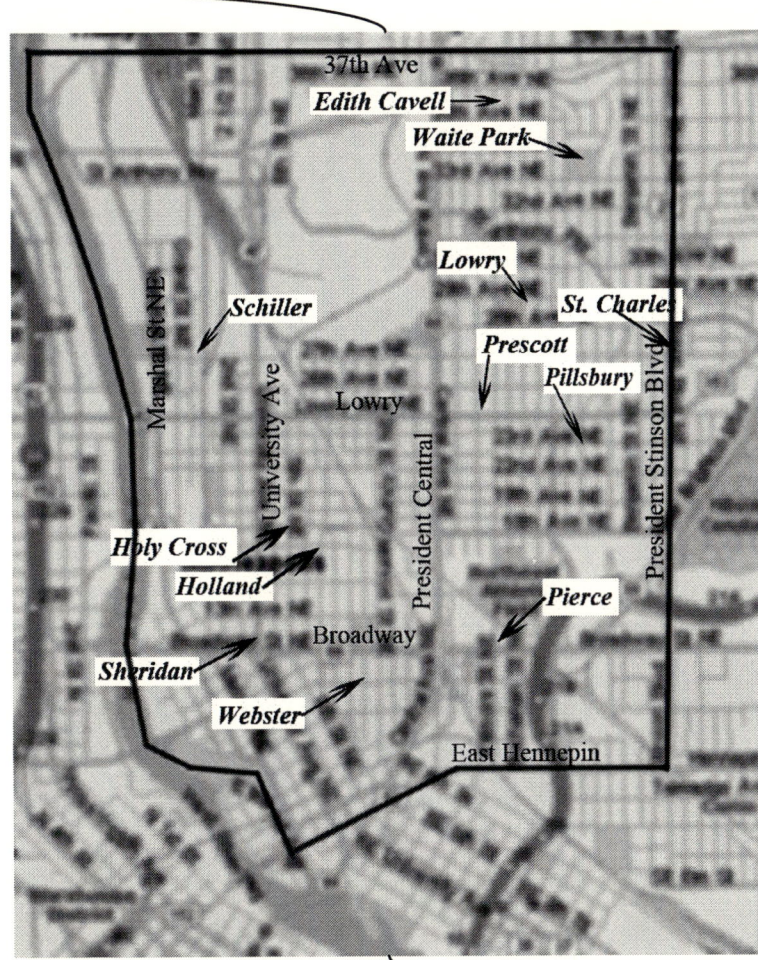

Gordie Solz

Big Fish in a Little Pond — Best of all was being a 6th grader in Prescott School. That year everyone bonded and enjoyed being the oldest in the school. We were in charge! Hall Monitors, Stair Captains, Patrols and of course teachers helpers! A great year and a good preparation for going to Edison High. Teachers were careful to work with us, always telling us we were the big kids now and to make sure we knew how to get along in a bigger school. Prescott was a neighborhood school supported by the community, and the children that were in school together also lived close to each other and played together as well.
Sandy Cederstrom Rorem

Little Fish in a Big Pond — Growing up in upper Nordeast, I went to Waite Park Grade School and was part of the second ever class to graduate from that august academe. But, in 1952, there was no North East Junior High. All of us from Waite Park, Pillsbury, and Schiller grade schools spent our first year of junior high school at Edison, which was then a Junior/Senior High School. After spending several years becoming the biggest fish in the littlest ponds, we suddenly became a part of a school with a population in excess of 2,000

(Continued on page 225)

CHAPTER ELEVEN — CLASS BACKWARDS

(Continued from page 224)

students and staff members.

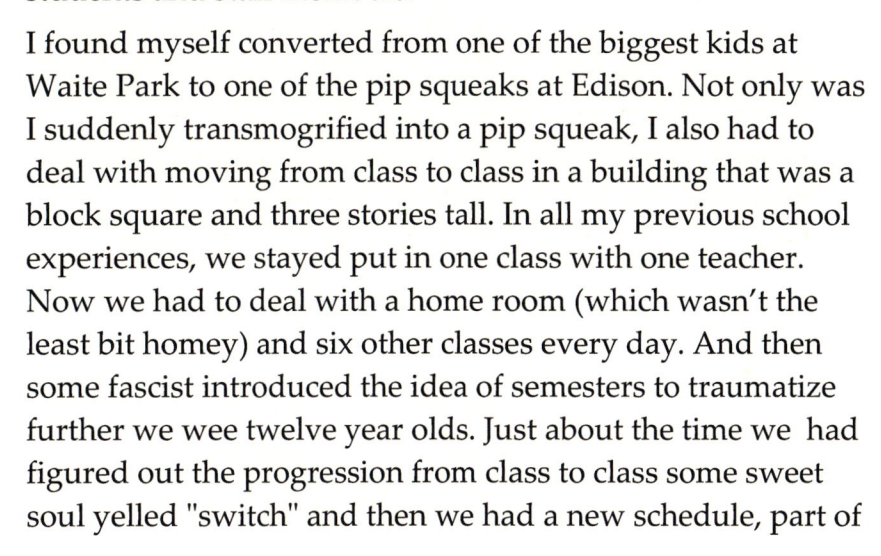

I found myself converted from one of the biggest kids at Waite Park to one of the pip squeaks at Edison. Not only was I suddenly transmogrified into a pip squeak, I also had to deal with moving from class to class in a building that was a block square and three stories tall. In all my previous school experiences, we stayed put in one class with one teacher. Now we had to deal with a home room (which wasn't the least bit homey) and six other classes every day. And then some fascist introduced the idea of semesters to traumatize further we wee twelve year olds. Just about the time we had figured out the progression from class to class some sweet soul yelled "switch" and then we had a new schedule, part of which was the same as it was and part was brand new. Someone said to me, "Oh, that's simple, Larry, we are now in the second semester, and you have music instead of gym and wood shop in place of metal crafts."

"What da ya mean, simple? I haven't gotten used to changing classes every 55 minutes yet, let alone swapping wood working for basket weaving – or was it the other way round?"

(Continued on page 226)

225

(Continued from page 225)

It was carefully explained to me that semesters were one half of the year and so there were two equal semesters. Good! That must mean one half school, and one half vacation, I could go for that. It was not to be. Both halves of the year were school halves and I began to fret over the loss of summer vacation.

Somewhere in the midst of this mind numbing new experience called Junior High I ended up stopping in the lavatory (it took me nearly a semester to learn that was the room you used when you found it necessary to relieve yourself) after lunch and prior to my fourth hour class. When I went in it seemed as though the room was filled with some very big, very boisterous upper classmen. I went and found myself a corner at the urinal and had just started my business when there was a sudden exodus from the room. Not just the upper class men, but everyone – sans Larry. Then as I stood there wondering what I'd done to screw things up now, a cherry bomb exploded. Ever been in a tiled room full of china fixtures when an explosion went off? The only soft thing in that whole room to absorb the sound was yours truly. For the next three periods, my friends kept telling me to zip my pants. It would have been nice if I could have heard any of them. **Larry Kohout**

Staying in one school — I went to Sheridan from kindergarten through 9th grade, 1945 through 1955. It's really unusual to be at one school for so long; not many schools offered that. It was great for forming long term friendships. In fact I still know and communicate with nine people that I met in kindergarten. After 9th grade, in 1955, my Sheridan classmates and I made the big move to Edison as sophomores. It was both scary and neat. Scary because of moving out of my comfort zone of friends and environment I'd known for many years and neat because I got to meet new friends and have many great experiences. **Louie Paff**

Not Such a Bad Kid —

1. In 7th and 8th grades I went to Sheridan.
    a. Snuck over to the bakery for some good rolls
    b. I had to be home at 9 pm on school nights and 12 pm on Saturday
    c. Did not destroy other people's property
    d. My hair style at Sheridan was a duck tail.
2. Met Jim Moore there and found out he lived a couple of blocks from me on Central and Summer Streets.
3. Had no problem with other people from different areas.

Ray Miller

L-M-N-O-P — Some of us came to Edison in the 7th grade, but many more came along later. This provided a constant opportunity to meet new friends. It recently occurred to me that disproportionately my friends and acquaintances from high school have last names starting with L or M or N (Dave Larson / Jean Midthun / Sharon Matt / Rod Nelson / etc). It was apparently easier to get to know people who were seated next to you alphabetically. Sometimes I wonder how different my life would be, if I knew more people with names starting with 'A' or 'Z'. **Dick Myslajek**

Echoes of the Fifties — The early fifties were a time of innocence, honesty, and integrity. Also, it was a time of respect for our elders and that included our parents and our teachers.
We could go to school and feel that we were safe. There was respect for discipline. It was a time for oneness: one TV, one car, one phone. **Jean Torgerson Strong**

| CHAPTER ELEVEN | CLASS BACKWARDS |

But life was not always perfect. There were snags along the way. For some of us, family tensions split us apart and life was not as simple as the "Ozzie and Harriet" kind of sit-coms. Our fresh young minds began to bump into a bigger world of happenings not so much noticed in our early years and rattled some "family" concepts. Polio at its peak in the beginning years some of our classmates. Because of the new threat of the atomic bomb in the '50s, the Korean conflict, and Joe McCarthy, the fear of Communism was brought to the forefront. Juvenile Delinquency was becoming a more frequent problem.

And We Became Aware

Rare Divorces — I was born and raised in Northeast on 24th and Polk Street. My parents divorced when my father came home from World War II and that is why I didn't live with both parents. At that time, my parents didn't want us to change schools and my Dad my Aunt Fern and Uncle Roland, so that's where I lived most of the time as well. Actually from age 8, I spent about half of my time living with them and the other half with my paternal grandmother. I went to Prescott School from kindergarten through 6th grade and then

(Continued on page 230)

(Continued from page 229)

Edison from 7th to 12th grade. I was up there on Arthur Street pretty much from 1948 but I didn't connect with the neighborhood pals until I came to Edison. That was somewhat difficult at that time, but Fern and Roland were not only parents to me, but wonderful grandparents to my children. They couldn't have done more or been more loving. They lived a long life both living well into their '90s. After we lost Roland, Fern moved to Washington with us and I had the privilege of being with her and caring for her until she passed. She died in our home and our entire family loved her and was grateful for every minute we had with her. Northeast Minneapolis was a special place in the '40s and '50s for sure. **Sandy Cederstrom Rorem**

The Age of the Silent Dysfunctional Family — The roles of mother-father in hindsight were really pretty clear in the 1940's. Dad would hold the job or jobs and earn the money. He expected the house to be kept clean, meals together (although I don't think there was ever any thought of

(Continued on page 231)

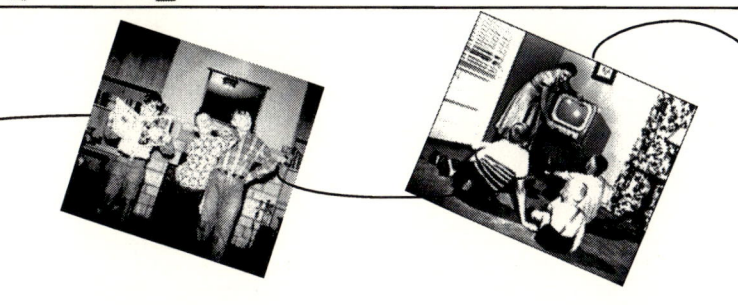

(Continued from page 230)

anyone eating without the other family members). But we had our differences too. When Dad was home, needing sleep, all were to be quiet. Mother's role was to raise the kids, clothe, feed, and clean them. We were in a sense her kids—at least from my eyes as the oldest. We did what we were told. There were no discussions or conversations about things we were doing. Mother was too busy keeping house, preparing meals, or getting us off to bed so she could have time to rest. Only later as teens did we start questioning or arguing over expectations only to be told, "That's the way your dad wants it." He earned the money, gave her an amount, which she became skilled at making last and providing for us. It always seemed strange to me to see friends talk with their parents. I grew up never really knowing that kids and parents actually talked to each other. I must have talked to them but still thought it strange to see others doing such. **Rod Nelson**

Glasses (aka Four-Eyes) — I thought I had

good vision as a small child. However, in third grade, either genetics or my new-found favored skill of reading caught up with me and my vision went very fuzzy. I had trouble reading the blackboard even from a second or third row seat. The school nurse or itinerant vision examiner consulted my folks and I remember going by bus to an eye clinic with my mother. After extreme dilation (which of course made my vision even worse), I was examined and fitted with new glasses which took some getting used to. The only other thing I remember was another kid who was also there to get glasses, ironically a girl from the same class (I don't remember her name). I remember us wandering around the waiting room, almost blind, guiding each other until the dilation wore off. I guess my sight was so bad that the only reason I recognized her the next day in class was that she also was wearing new glasses.

Even though I had to survive the usual taunts and teasing ("four-eyes, blind as a bat," etc.), I appreciated my new acute vision but glasses always seemed to be in the way. Somewhere in that 5 year period, all four members of my family

(Continued on page 233)

(Continued from page 232)

ended up with glasses, bifocals for my parents. I was not endowed with any great athletic skills, but wearing glasses further squelched many athletic activities. I even tried playing basketball on my church team without glasses but that was a dismal failure.

Later, I developed enough of a degree of fitness to participate in some sports. I played church league softball, alley basketball, and sandlot touch football having taught myself to pass and punt. Sure would have been even more fun if I hadn't had to wear glasses.   **Bob Buntrock**

Polio - Epidemics of Fear and Paralysis—

Throughout the 1940's and the first half of the 1950's, polio was an ever-increasing threat. A lack of understanding about the disease was partly due to fund raising efforts of the March of Dimes. Poster children, shown in braces or in iron lungs, generated pity to raise cash for survivors and research. The disease clearly impacted behavior. People avoided crowds whenever possible and stayed away from public swimming pools and beaches.

In late August, 1953, while playing football I developed a headache. Prone to migraine headaches, I simply went home,

(Continued on page 234)

(Continued from page 233)

took two aspirin, and went to bed. But the headache got worse. I developed a severe stiffness in my back and neck. I felt as though something was trying to twist me backwards into a circle. My problems increased for several more days and until finally a doctor diagnosed me with "polio." An ambulance took me to the Sister Kenny Institute in Minneapolis. I was placed on a table, rolled, my head near my knees, so that they could perform a spinal tap. As they inserted the needle into my spine, my mother passed out, I assume, due to the fear she was experiencing.

On September 1st, 1953, the day I was hospitalized, Doctor Jonas Salk successfully developed a vaccine that would prevent people from contracting polio. (Strange that you <u>catch</u> a cold, and <u>catch</u> the flu, but you <u>contract</u> polio.) Too late for me. I was diagnosed with spinal bulbar polio encephalitis. I don't remember much until I woke over a week later lying in an iron lung. My legs were both chunks of immoveable meat. My back – which still felt as though it was turning me into a donut – wouldn't react to anything I wanted to do. I could feel secretions building in my throat, but I couldn't move them. I overheard a doctor saying that if I didn't improve shortly he would have to perform a tracheotomy.

(Continued on page 235)

(Continued from page 234)

I began to work the secretions up and swallow them. This is a fairly normal process but I had to learn to swallow and breathe over again. Overcoming these simple but huge hurdles, was just the beginning of what I had to relearn.

Not only could I not walk, I couldn't even sit up unaided. When the fever subsided, they declared I was no longer infectious and could be out of the iron lung. They started hot packing me. Each limb was wool-wrapped and encased in insulating rubber. Then the real work began.

Polio survivors who endured the Sister Kenny treatment remember the smell of the hot wet wool and the packs as hurting. My recollection is of minor pain as I was first wrapped with wool but the heat of the wool caused a relaxation in the muscle and relieved the pain of the contraction. Packed three times a day, we would then be taken to physical therapy immediately after the packs were removed.

Therapy consisted of stretching out muscle contractions and tendons to allow voluntary functioning beginning the process of innervation. Polio doesn't simply kill nerves, but often it would just damage them. After a period of recovery, as nerves awakened or sprouted, I began to be able to sit up on

(Continued on page 236)

March of Dimes poster child, 1949:
Linda Brown

March of Dimes poster child, 1948:
Terry Tullos

(Continued from page 235)

my own. Later they taught me to stand and, finally, to start walking with the aid of crutches and braces. When I left the hospital in May of 1954, I was walking, albeit with an unsteady and limping gait, but also without crutches or braces. My mother and grandmother continued the therapy at home until I achieved a fairly steady gait.

When September 1, 1954 arrived, I started ninth grade with a barely noticeable hitch in my giddyup and I had ceased blaming others for my problems. What they didn't teach us as part of the hospital routine was how *not* to be ashamed of what had happened to us. Since there was such a fear of polio in the world, we naturally tried to hide any disability.

As I grew, the muscle in my left leg did not. I walked by hyper-extending my knee to keep it from collapsing. By my mid-20s, I started wearing a brace on that leg and soon needed a corset to support my weak back muscles. Things stayed that way until the onset of post-polio syndrome some 20 years later. The epidemics of fear and paralysis were ended in the industrialized world by the Salk and Sabin vaccines. By the time we, the class of 1958, were having our children, polio was virtually unheard of in the US. But the stigma that so many of us felt took a while longer to heal.   **Larry Kohout**

March of Dimes poster child, 1950: Wanda Wiley

March of Dimes poster child, 1952: Larry Jim Gross against the backdrop of the Korean War

The Korean conflict — The advent of the Cold War hung over all of us. We were sending our own "Care Packages" to our relatives in Germany and although none of them lived in Berlin, the Berlin Blockade depressed us as the airlift uplifted us. Further developments in atomic and hydrogen bombs renewed scares of attacks. I don't remember when we started doing under-the-desk bomb drills in schools, but they became part of our school lives. The Cold War became hotter when South Korea was invaded in June of 1950.
Bob Buntrock

Fear Of The Bomb — At the beginning of The Korean conflict, (1950) while the Soviet Union was testing their nuclear devices, a fear of Communism spread over the United States. Senator Joe McCarthy inflamed this fear by his accusations that Communists had infiltrated our government and the entertainment business. The fear grew to such proportions that the Federal Civil Defense Administration produced a film for school children telling us what to do in case of a nuclear attack: We were advised to get under a table or huddle against a wall in a fetal position, covering our heads with our hands to protect us from harm.   **Carol Lyons Larson**

Not Quite So Safe — To quickly summarize, we were incredibly free compared to kids nowadays to explore and learn on our own without undue worry/concern from our parents. Ours was a simpler and seemingly safer time. Part of that freedom was because the mass media of communications was relative primitive compared to now, and parents didn't hear about the abductions and other horrible things we now hear of.

But those abductions did happen. I had a personal experience with that. When I was maybe 8 or 9 I walked the six blocks to East Hennepin. Two older youth, probably in their late teens, latched onto me, and made me go with them. I remember that they were up to no good, and I was becoming really scared.

At about University Avenue and 1st Street Northeast, near the streetcar barns, I made a panicky run for it. I ran east along 1st Street for about two blocks until I tired, and they caught up with me. I then had to walk north on University Avenue with them. Going over the bridge over the railroad tracks we passed two women walking south. The guys told me to go snatch one of the women's purses. Being totally scared I approached one of the women. She yelled at me and I quickly retreated. I was forced to walk north with them until about 6th Avenue. At that point they lost interest in me and allowed me to take off. With huge relief I ran home (less than a block) and told my parents what had happened. They were totally upset about it, but didn't think to call the police. I've always felt fortunate that that was the extent of my abduction. **Louie Paff**

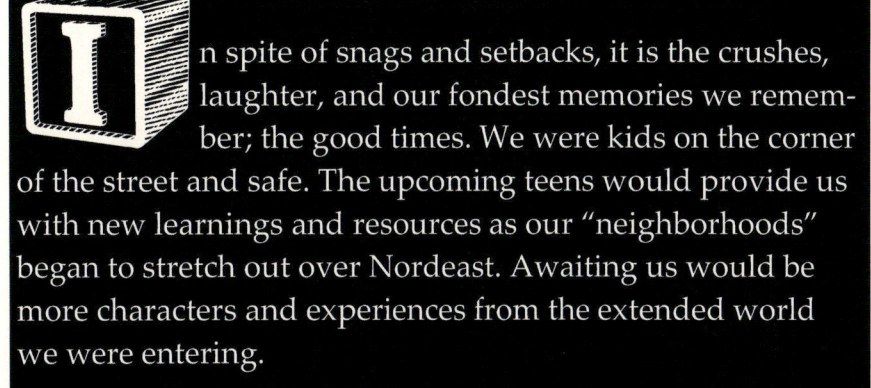

Lasting Pictures of the Past

In spite of snags and setbacks, it is the crushes, laughter, and our fondest memories we remember; the good times. We were kids on the corner of the street and safe. The upcoming teens would provide us with new learnings and resources as our "neighborhoods" began to stretch out over Nordeast. Awaiting us would be more characters and experiences from the extended world we were entering.

Our *"Class Backwards"* trip ends. But just as any good conversation begins to wind down, there will always be those comments like:

> Yah but…
> How about the…
> Oh, I gotta tell ya…

And so we add on the following to give you one last look…

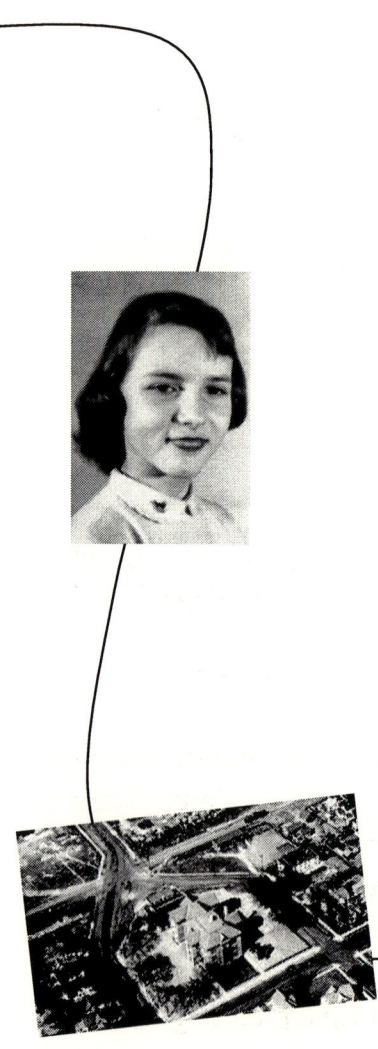

Our First Crushes

Carvings on a Wall — The PNA (Polish National Alliance) was housed above the drug store. You always knew when there was a party or a wedding reception there, because the lights hanging from the ceiling in Rolig's would sway with the dancing on second floor. It was fascinating – and scary to be in the drug store at those times and watch the wild movement of the lights while the guests upstairs were doing the polka.

The wall on the 4th Street side of the drug store was dark red brick with no windows. We used it as a free billboard to advertise and announce items from our young, active lives. We carved our names and the names of those we were romantically involved, or wanted to be romantically involved with, complete with big plus signs or hearts sporting arrows through them. When the romances cooled, the carvings stayed on for all to see, sometimes with laughter, sometimes with sighs – like a history book opened to a previous page.
Carolyn Jodie Hagford

My Brilliant Idea — When I was a school patrol, I had a huge crush on Darryl Bourgerie, another classmate who was a patrol. I kept thinking of ways I could get him to notice me. Then I had this brilliant idea. I had been taking tap-dancing lessons at MacPhail. One day, after we were done helping the little kids walk safely across the street, I came over to him and started tap-dancing. He didn't even notice. Speaking of crushes, I was crushed. So then I walked over to another boy in our class and started tap dancing as we walked back to school. He didn't notice either. I thought I would never have much success with boys. I was even going to quit going to school dances because no one asked me to dance. My girlfriends persuaded me to go to the dances anyway. They needed someone to hold their purses. **Bev Warren**

Ladies Choice — I had a mad crush on Marion Baarstad in 7th grade at Sheridan. She was really cute, different from any of the girls I knew from Pierce. One problem: she was a year older than me. I needed to do something to make her notice me…I sat on our front porch several times that summer thinking, "How does an immature 14-year-old impress a really cute 15-year-old?" I thought up a plan to get her to notice me…

(Continued on page 242)

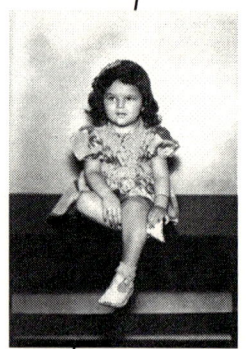

(Continued from page 241)

I knew that she walked to school on Broadway from Monroe, right by Ambles soda fountain. And, I rode my bike down Broadway to school. My plan: I would ride down Broadway close to Monroe and watch for her coming to the corner. When she did, I would start riding my bike and let go of the handlebars, being very cool, and ride right down in front her. She couldn't help but notice me…no hands!

One morning, I saw Marion coming to the corner. I began peddling on my brand-new red Schwinn Cruiser, no hands…I was looking cool! Just as I came to the corner, my pants leg got caught in the bicycle chain. My Cruiser screeched and skidded on the street gravel to an instant stop and tipped over, me crumpled underneath it with my pants leg ripped up to my knee…not cool!

My plan sort of worked…she sure did notice me! Later, I thought to myself, there goes any chance of her liking me. But I was wrong. Because, when it was "ladies choice" at the next Friday night dance, she asked me to dance….I was in heaven. A really cute girl a year older and 6 inches taller than me wanted to dance with me. My monster crush, Marion Baarstad, became my first puppy love. I truly was cool! **Bobby Peters**

Puppy Love — The first girl I ever kissed was Mary Lou Long on the playground. I think the girls had more crushes on boys. It was kind of a puppy love thing. **Ray Miller**

Our Fondest Memories

How lucky we were to have lived in an era when we could gather at night at the band concert in Windom Park; to walk for miles in the snow after dark, and feel the fresh, crisp snow on our tongue and make an occasional angel in the snow; to ride our bikes throughout Northeast and beyond, and had no one worry about where we were or our safety; to have hours of unstructured play time outside that we ourselves organized including piles of leaves to jump in, snow forts to build, and neighborhood games to play as the sun was setting and the smell of fall was in the air.
Mary Ann Tema Weinberger

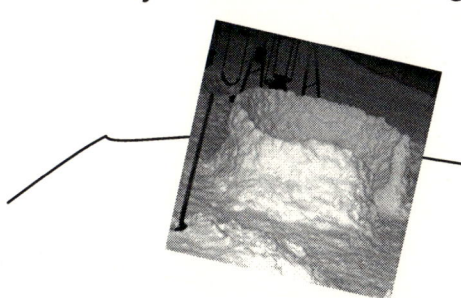

CLASS BACKWARDS — CHAPTER ELEVEN

The best memory for me was having the freedom to go play wherever we wanted without constant adult supervision. The only expectation was to be in by dark.   **Louie Paff**

The best summers were the ones I spent with all my cousins at my grandmother's cabin.   **Larry Kohout**

One of my prize memories was going to the Sheridan Library and being able to take out six books at a time. What joy! I got my first taste of the Yellow Fairy Tale book, the Green Fairy Tale book, on and on through all the colors.
Carolyn Jodie Hagford

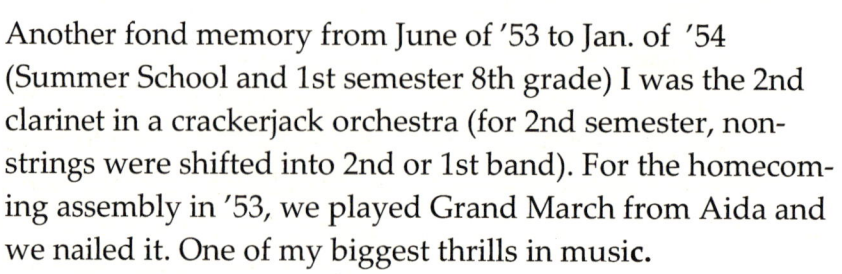

Another fond memory from June of '53 to Jan. of '54 (Summer School and 1st semester 8th grade) I was the 2nd clarinet in a crackerjack orchestra (for 2nd semester, non-strings were shifted into 2nd or 1st band). For the homecoming assembly in '53, we played Grand March from Aida and we nailed it. One of my biggest thrills in music.
Bob Buntrock

My parents taught me to take care of what was important to me. They bought me a blue bike, which I rode all over Nordeast and many times out to Lake Johanna and Lake Josephine. I even rode it to school on occasion. I loved that bike, washing it and shining it frequently. When I no longer needed it, the bike was as nice as it was at the beginning. Guess who bought it? Mr. Acko, my wonderful sixth grade teacher at Pillsbury! **Jean Torgerson Strong**

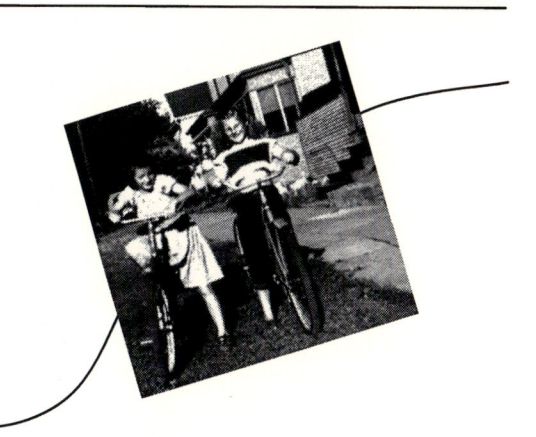

I remember getting sick in school and having to walk home vomiting along the way. Parents didn't have an extra car to pick you up. Mother's skills really came out when one of us four kids got sick. Not just a cold, but bedridden diseases like measles, mumps, and flu. We were treated to breakfast on a tray in bed each morning as well as the other meals. They were specially made of oatmeal, juices, soups, peanut butter and jelly. A paper bag carefully folded open sat alongside the bed for emergencies. Every few days the sheets were changed and you crawled in between fresh ones just in from outside lines. Almost anything you wanted she got for you, but it basically was a few books and coloring books. There were no extra radios for you to have and TV was out of the question. Lots of loving care via temperature taking and even a small sponge bath was had. Funny thing, that in all the years of growing up, I don't remember Mother ever being sick. She must have been so when we weren't looking. **Rod Nelson**

My best memories of grade school days were recess. I got an "A." The five years I spent in sixth grade were the best years of my life. I also fondly remember chasing little red-haired girls around the school parking lot. **Dennis Olsen**

In two all-school plays, I was Cinderella in 4th grade and waltzed with two Prince Charmings, Norm Solberg and Jeff McCune, and in 6th grade, I was the Pied Piper of Hamline. I really did enjoy walking back and forth from school with my pal Ron Willow and going home for lunch and will always remember a magical night of skating with Dennis Olsen. I have other outstanding memories of Audrey's cabin with the girls and Windom Park band concerts. **Carol Lyons Larson**

I just remember how much I loved skating at Audubon Park in the winter after leaving School (Thomas Lowry).
Athena Dascalos

Once I started skating (not until age 10), my fondest memories were walking the 3 blocks to the Windom rink (when homework was done, of course), the feeling of freedom while skating (and the smell of wet wool mittens drying on the wood stove), and literally coming back to earth when done (my feet felt like lead the whole way home).
Bob Buntrock

CHAPTER ELEVEN — CLASS BACKWARDS

The first hollow at Audubon Park was for skating, like a depression, then the warming house, then the second hollow used for hockey & speed skating. There was a big hill on the south you could slide down to the 2nd hollow..... it's all gone now. **Judy Sheldon Johnson**

The wonderful soda fountain at the drugstore on 29th and Johnson where you could get homemade ice cream and butterscotch sundaes with whipped cream for twenty cents; and getting out of school early and riding the streetcar to the Shrine Circus at the auditorium where the vendors sold live chameleons and Turkish taffy. I'd still like to buy a chameleon. **Mary Lou Kranak Cheleen**

I remember the teachers, they were so interested in us and I felt like I knew them all personally. That was very much the case during 7, 8 and 9th grade. We were young to be in the high school, so I suspect they paid special attention to us kids who came from K-6. They cared about how we learned and encouraged us to stretch. They were our mentors and I especially remember that we began to learn the political process by electing student government, campaigning, and helping our "candidates" win. The teachers acted as advisors

(Continued on page 248)

CLASS BACKWARDS   CHAPTER · ELEVEN

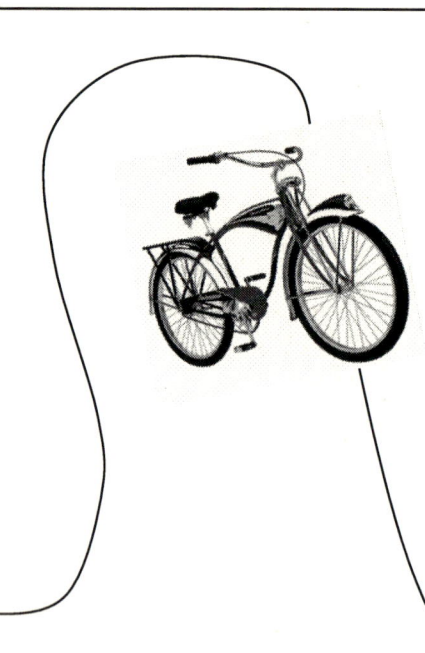

(Continued from page 247)

and under their wing, we enjoyed the work of a campaign. Ron Willow for President!

At the end of the year, we had a celebration for graduation. We received a purple and gold ribbon and a bow that was about a 2 feet long. We wore it on our waist and everyone in the class signed their name – sort of like the yearbook. The rage was quilted skirts, bobby sox and baby doll saddle shoes. We square danced for the 6th grade party and all the parents came to watch!

Sandy Cederstrom Rorem

Chapter Eleven — Class Backwards

What started out as a fun conversation became a project; a book that would end up taking three years to produce and involve more than 50 authors. Mark Twain once said if he had more time, he would've written a shorter book. We think if we had more time, we would've written a longer book! There are many people we could not reach. We tried to correct any factual mistakes, but then this is a book of memories, not facts. These are our memories of the era because we lived it. They are not complete. There will be, of course, memories we missed somewhere along the road that may pop back into view about the Nordeast we all loved the most. Nevertheless, enjoy what we found, share them, relive them, and do so to the fullest.

And we do agree: Nordeast Is Beautiful!

CLASS BACKWARDS

CHAPTER · ELEVEN

Edison Authors

1. Arone, Mike
2. Buntrock, Bob
3. Cederstrom Rorem, Sandy
4. Coveney Fields, Kathleen
5. Dascalos, Athena
6. Decker Johnson, Bev
7. Erpelding, Loren
8. Grivna Peters, Penny
9. Halverson, Dale
10. Hudoba Rosenberger, Claire
11. Jodie Hagford, Carolyn
12. Knutsen, Dodd
13. Kocon, Ed
14. Kohanik, Joe
15. Kohout, Larry #
16. Kondrak, Jerry
17. Kranak Cheleen, Mary
18. Larson, David #
19. Larson, Norman
20. Lewacko Yantos, Nadia
21. Lohn, Pete
22. Lyons Larson, Carol #
23. Lyons, Red
24. Mandery, Wayne
25. Matt Weglinski, Sharon
26. Midthun Olsen, Judy
27. Miller, Ray
28. Miskowiec, Anweiler, Janet
29. Mrozka Mros, Janet
30. Myslajek Godava, Pat
31. Myslajek, Dick #
32. Nelson, Rod #
33. Olsen, Dennis
34. Olson Tanner, Nancy
35. Paff, Louie
36. Peters, Bobby
37. Rau, Joanne
38. Schleisman Booth, Ann
39. Sexton Lubrecht, Marilyn
40. Sheldon Johnson, Judy
41. Sherwood, Richard
42. Simon Erickson, Ginny
43. Solberg, Norm #
44. Solz, Gordie
45. Tema Weinberger, Mary Ann
46. Terry, Jim
47. Torgerson Strong, Jean #
48. Urista, Tom
49. Vandermyde, John
50. Walker Mandery, Sue
51. Warren, Bev
52. Watten, Dana
53. Wiggen Monette, Anita
54. Willow, Ron

= Edison Authors committee member

Title	Page
Edison High School	1
The Committee l to r Dave Larson, Rod Nelson, Jean Torgerson, Dick Myslajek, Norm Solberg, Larry Kohout, Carol Larson.	1
Red, Bev, and Carol Lyons	2
Edison in the oval	2
Rod Nelson in his mother's arms	2
Sharron Matt in her mother's arms	2
Nordeast outline map (L Kohout collage)	3
Bird's eye 1872 drawing looking across river at Minneapolis from the St. Anthony side (Now Northeast and Southeast Minneapolis	4
Lunch bag and apple	5
Hollywood Theater	6
Butcher with revised signs as seen in Myslajek's Bar (N Solberg drawing)	7
Nordeast is beautiful button	8
Larson boys	9
Stocked shelves	10
Waffles and Bacon	10
Backyard chickens	11
Footed pajamas	11
Treadle sewing machine	11
Oval braided rug	12
Margarine poster	12
Coin purse	13
Solz food delivery truck (substitute)	13
Leggings and post cards	14
Athena Dascalos's father	15
Blue star service flag (L Kohout collage)	15
Waste fats sign on butcher's counter	15
Troop train interior	16
Troop train exterior	16
Rod Nelson and his aunt	16
Polly and Penny Grivna with their aunt	16
Buy War Bonds poster	17
Table top radio	17
Rod Nelson's uncle	18
Mary Ann Tema's Lamb (substitute)	18
Tin foil ball	19
Rod Nelson's grandfather	19
1941 Chevrolet	19
Kids at play (C Kohout drawing)	20
Black out	21
Photo of celebration at end of WWII	21
Hobos (N Solberg drawing)	22
Steam whistles (L Kohout collage)	22
Grandma Babushka (N Solberg drawing)	23
Map of Czechoslovakia	24

Title	Page
Map of Germany	25
Map of Sweden	25
Map of Greece	26
Map of Lebanon	26
Map of Italy	28
Map of Poland	29
Grandpa & Grandma ?? with the twins	30
Map of Slovakia	31
Map of Russia	32
Nadia Lewacko'a birth certificate	32
Nadia and Helen Lewacko at camp in West Germany	33
Tamera, Helen & Nadia Lewacko	33
Nadia and family in front of "one room shack" in West Germany	34
Map of Nordeast churches	35
Sign post of Nordeast Nationalities (N Solberg drawing)	36
Please Sign In & Out Birth Death Register (R Nelson drawing)	37
St. John's Evangelical Lutheran Church	37
Confirmation Class in German Only (R Nelson drawing)	38
St. Mathew's Episcopal Church Lowry at the corner of Fillmore - Courtesy Hennepin County Library, Special Collections	39

Title	Page
Four Churches on one Block - a world record?	40
Wayne Mandery climbing out window (R Nelson drawing)	41
Soup dish for discipline of bad language	42
Jean Torgerson in her light blue dotted Swiss	43
Bishop Sheen on cover of TV Guide	44
St Cyril and Methodius Church at 13th Ave NE and 2nd St.	44
Boy teaching Carolyn Jodie swear words (R Nelson drawing	45
Holy Bible	46
Rod in his communion clothes	47
Church piano vignette	48
Running from hell (R Nelson drawing)	49
Pea shooters	49
Nun lecturing boys	50
Bag of peanuts photo	50
Trinity Methodist Church Confirmation Class	51
St. Paul's Lutheran Confirmation Class	51
Hell and Damnation preaching (R Nelson drawing)	52
Bottle of homemade wine	53
Young Boy Bowling	53
Grandma O'Rourke	55

Title	Page
Christmas program music (L Kohout collage)	56
Flutes	57
Easter food basket	57
Pascha Bread	58
A section of the pipes in Louie Paff's pipe organ	58
Catholic num (N Solberg drawing)	59
Wedding Photos from the Sharon Matt Collection	59
Wedding Photo of dancing from the Sharon Matt Collection	60
Shivaree pot and pan covers	60
An Angelic Bob Buntrock	61
An Angelic Louie Paff	61
Neighborhood kids 1: Dale Halverson, Jim Terry, Dick Myslajek, Gary Pierson, Dodd Knutsen, Owen Green, Dennis Terry, Mickey Graham	63
Neighborhood kids and cover photo: Front row - L to R Tom Scales, Tom Graham, Betty Kay Neeb, Ted Lukaska, Lynn Knutsen, Mickey Graham, John Scales Back row - l to r Dodd Knutsen, Dick Myslajek, Carol Bender, Jim Terry, Dale Halverson, Dennis Terry	63
Karen Kleshold, Rod Nelson, Jean Torgerson	63
Roller skates and skate key (R Cunningham drawings)	64
Margaret Barry House, 759 Pierce Street	65
Looks like hide & seek	65
Delmonico's Italian Foods	65
Bob Buntrock's House on 19th Ave. The Place I Will Always Call Home	66
Fritz Adler (Grounds Keeper) Feeding the Salvation Army Camp Deer - Courtesy of Hennepin County Library, Special Collections	66
Salvation Army Camp Goats with Fritz Adler (Grounds Keeper) Courtesy of Hennepin County Library, Special Collections	67
Jax Café sign	67
Little Jack's Steak House sign	68
Wall outside the Little Sisters of The Poor On Broadway between 2nd & 3rd Ave.	68
Child in front of Little Sisters Wall circa 1945	69
One of the House in the Valley	70
A Pysanky Egg	70
One of the House on the Hill 32nd & McKinley (from back)	70
The Gypsy?	71
Jean Torgerson and the Dog	71
The Ragman	72
Horse Drawn Dairy Wagon - Courtesy of Hennepin County Library Special Collections	73

Title	Page
Dick Myslajek's House on the Hill	74
When We Still Had Elms	75
Carol Lyons Home of Stability	76
Marilyn Sexton sitting on the culverts in the North Star Company yard	77
A Northeast Four-plex	79
Louie's wooden peach crate	80
Octopus forced air furnace	81
Shoveling coal	81
The Semanko & Larson Duplex	82
Street grading – one of summer's excitements	83
Quonset huts at 1500 Buchanan St. Northeast, Minneapolis, 1946. Image courtesy of the Minnesota Historical Society	83
Cherry Angel Food Cake – Food for the gods and she was paid by the devils.	84
Johnny cakes—buttered - the heathens	84
With beans you could find both yellow (wax) and green in the same vegetable	85
Dial telephone - Do you remember? They really did look like this.	86
Reacher used in the corner store to bring boxes from high shelves (R Nelson drawing)	86
Basement hot water furnace – One of the Monsters	87
Coal Truck Ready to Deliver a Season's Worth of Coal (Photo courtesy of www.fidelitybs.com)	87
Combination wood burning and gas stove	88
Saturday night at the tub	88

Title	Page
Snug as a bug – (C Kohout drawing)	89
The Church Pair (L Kohout photo collage	89
Mittens on a string (I Cunningham drawing)	90
Never far away, the mending basket	90
Unidentified men working on their "Victory Garden"	92
Mrs. Nelson at her garden	93
The rooster crows in the hood (I Cunningham drawing)	93
Preparing for dinner (the baby chicks)	94
This is as close as you are going to get to seeing the duck's neck slit	94
Tomatoes in the pressure cooker	94
Shullo's Leaf Grocery	95
Boy pulling wagon full of groceries	95
Witt's downtown market - Courtesy Hennepin County Library, Special Collections	96
Soda bottle caps (L Kohout photo collage)	97
Wax soda bottles /Bazooka bubble gum/candy necklace/was mustache. (L Kohout photo collage)	98
Candy cigarettes (L Kohout photo collage)	99
Barqs Crème Soda bottle (R Nelson Photo	100
Blackey's Bakery	100
Artisan Breads (L Kohout photo collage)	100
Pastries (L Kohout photo collage)	101
Marble sundae	101
Ready's Meats sign	101

Title	Page
National Tea Story	102
Howdy Doody cookie jar	102
Filled grocery bag	103
Mother's grocery list	103
Woman reaching into ice box	104
A white oak ice box	104
A horse drawn ice wagon	105
Ice tongs lifting an ice cube	105
An ice thief	106
Milkman setting milk at the back door	106
Gallon milk bottle of the era	106
Cardboard "Need Ice Today" sign	107
Family sitting around supper table (I & S Cunningham drawing)	107
Father and child napping together after supper	108
Back yard picnic table (I Cunningham drawing)	108
Woman hanging clothes outside	108
Hand cranked clothes wringer	109
Clothes hanging in basement	109
Racking & burning leaves (R Nelson Photo)	109
Young child trying to push a mower	110
7 ounce Coke bottle`	110
Wooden box that stored charge receipts	111

Title	Page
Charge record book	111
Back and front of popsicle	111
Farm truck (I Cunningham drawing)	112
Children at play (L Kohout photo collage	113
Photo of a 1950 quarter	114
Kids on parade – from Sharron Matt Weglinski	114
Kids tobogganing	115
Kids playing kick the can	115
Boy in wagon	116
Steps	116
Carolyn Bak and Ralph Fuerst start nailing the siding on their shack. As shown in the October 1950 McCall's magazine	117
Harry Forsythe lays first sill before partner John Kraft finishes tough job of excavating in hard clay. As shown in the October 1950 McCall's magazine	118
Girls proved such good builders that early anti-feminist movement died out. Patty Kellerman, Patty Iverson and Diane Koelfgen start a house. As shown in the October 1950 McCall's magazine	119
Jimmy Barry finds he is up to using a man-size saw. He is one of more than 200 children that used the playground. As shown in the October 1950 McCall's magazine	119

Title	Page
Norm's street of mediation. Norm's house is on the left.	120
Curb and gutter laid through cow pasture as city expands north and east. Courtesy of the Minnesota Historical Society	120
Current photo of Kathleen Coveney Fields' home. The porch didn't exist in her times in the house	121
Muskrat trap	121
Jack 'O Lantern	122
Scary dark alley	122
An alley playground	123
Toy boat at the foot of St. Anthony Falls (L Kohout photo collage)	123
Skating on an icy downhill run (from Sharron Matt Weglinski)	124
Kids with skates, resting	124
Speed skates	125
Girls tightening skates	125
Black rubber boots (I Cunningham drawing)	125
Bumpy Ice Rink — How dumb were we?	126
Warming house stove	126
Pile of smelly socks (L Kohout photo collage)	127
Snow fort with a sled for a bed	127
Crack the whip – Saturday Evening Post cover	128
Sleigh Ride in Columbia Park - Image courtesy of the Minnesota Historical Society	128
Boys Throwing Snowballs at Girls (I Cummings drawing)	129
Snow angel in process	129
Saint Anthony Boulevard looking west	130
Start of a soap box derby race – And it begins	130
Three unidentified drivers in their mighty machines	131
Brown Bullhead Ameiurus nebulosus	131
Shooting marbles	132
Marbles including shooters and a steely	132
The swimming pool	132
John Ryan's Locker Room - Image courtesy of the Minnesota Historical Society	133
La Tarantella	133
Camden pool	134
Bobby Peters & the Knights of the Round Table	134
Scattered cards	135
Classics Illustrated - comic books	135
Scout camp – Troup 157	136
Six scouts	136
Lincoln Log	137
Games collage	137
Game of Authors	137

Title	Page
Erector Set advertisement	138
Back yard tent	138
Guns, holsters, scooters, and wagons	139
Bloody knife and Brownie Camera	140
Marilyn Sexton and family	141
A wedding in the Sexton family	141
Dolls	142
A tea set, set out	142
Banana layered white cake with fluffy white frosting	143
Wizard of Oz poster	145
National Velvet poster	145
Mickey Rooney movie promotional piece	145
Arion Theater	146
Ritz Theater	147
Roy Rogers	147
Milk Duds candy box	148
Hollywood Theater	148
Three views of the interior of the old Hollywood Theater as it appeared in our youth - Photos courtesy of Cinema Treasures http://cinematreasures.org/	149
Charlie Chan movie poster and still from one of the pictures	150
The Falcon Takes Over movie poster and Joe McDoakes poster	151
Post War Frazer (probably 1947) (C Kohout drawing)	152
Truck spraying DDT at a drive in movie theater	152
Ice Cream Cone drawing	153
Cars all lined up in a drive in theater	153
Lone Ranger with Silver	153
Family sitting together listening to the radio	154
Louies's diagram of his crystal set	154
Nicollet Base Ball Park	155
Buster Brown and his dog Tighe	155
Cedric Adams	156
News paper ads for radio shoes	156
Television test pattern	157
Tom Mix comic book cover	157
Vacuum tube tester and vacuum tubes (L Kohout photo collage	158
Captain Video poster	159
Muntz Console TV	159
Television listings from days gone by	160
Dial phone with Nordeast exchanges arrayed around dial (L Kohout photo collage)	160
Chuck Grissom and Lou Paff modeling Red Owl Uniforms for Aquatennial Parade	161
The 1949 combined Sheridan Band & Choir	161
A Windom Park bank concert song sheet	162

Title	Page
A pop corn wagon	163
Basement stairs where heads get wedged	164
Twisting in a tire swing until you get sick (I Cummings drawing)	164
Tongue stuck to the flag pole (I Cummings drawing)	164
Bandaged head of an over rocker (I Cummings drawing)	165
Glider that brought down concrete – or the other way	165
Bull dozers	166
Drowning hand ((I Cummings drawing)	167
ReddiWhip rocket ship	168
Hemorrhaging eye (C Kohout photo alteration)	168
Lobby of the Radio City Theater - Can you find Jerry, Joey, and Frankie?	169
US flag	171
Class room pledge of allegiance	171
Waite Park under construction - Courtesy of the Minnesota Historical Society	172
Central Avenue Library of the 1940s & '50s	172
Pillsbury School of the 1940s & '50s	173
Dyslexic writing	173
Cut the Pie	174
Game paraphernalia	174
Making dames down by the sewer	175

Title	Page
School bell	176
President Truman waves his hat to the crowd	176
Sheet music to Bell Bottom Trousers	177
Thomas Lowry of the '40s and '50s	177
A Valentine card	178
Watching film on crime and punishment	178
Sheets of Shubert's Unfinished Symphony	179
Lunch left on old fashioned school desk (L Kohout photo collage)	180
Lunch time playground game paraphernalia	180
Seven people who all attended the same kindergarten class	181
Mrs. Bachlor double exposed on her class	181
Mrs. Bachlor	182
Ten foot high snow banks (of memory)	183
Pierce School of the '40s & '50s – from the Bob Peters collection	183
Webster as we saw it.	184
Margaret Kranz with Sturdy and Sparkle	184
White rats	185
Students rushing to the circus via the streetcar	185
Fun fest poster	186
Kids bundling newspapers	186
Piles of papers – which room is the winner	187

Title	Page
Some of the paper sale extra bonus	187
Two students involved in the 1948 teachers strike	188
Sheridan on parade	189
Minnehaha Falls	189
School patrol crossing flag	189
Pig cutting board	190
Second grade math book	190
Welcome Travelers poster	191
The guy's view of dating	191
The girl's view of dating	191
Penny's in the Red Cross Jar	192
Hand in the kindergarten sand box	192
Second grade readers	193
Straight rows of seats in the elementary class	194
Clarinet and saxophone from grade school music lessons	194
Native with blow dart gun	195
Worn to a frazzle teacher	196
The intrepid Mrs. Bachlor	196
Street car coming off the Broadway bridge	197
Steam and smoke of the railroad	197
Douglas DC6 airliner	197
The end of a busy day of shopping or work. - Courtesy Minnesota Historical Society	198
Powers Department Store is to the right and Boutelle's Furniture to the left. - Courtesy Minnesota Historical Society	198
Streetcar at 27th and Washington - Courtesy Minnesota Historical Society	199
Donaldson's Department Store	199
Ecklund's Men's Clothing Store	200
Child hanging on the straps on the streetcar	200
Kids with heads out the window of the streetcar	201
Passengers getting off streetcars	201
Box of caps for cap gun	202
MacPhail School of Music	203
Streetcar stuck in the snow	203
Woolworth's Post Card	204
Out with the streetcars, here come the buses	204
Ripping up the streetcar rails	205
A train up close and personal	205
Someone had best tell the streetcar motorman that that is a train coming through the mill	206
The spike mauler	208
Two kids up close to a train	208
Smoke and steam of a steam engine	208
A scary railroad viaduct	209
The Monroe street viaduct	209
The Milwaukee Depot	210

Title	Page
A Pullman Ad from the period '42 to '48	210
A toy Pullman coach	210
Great Northern Depot	211
A hobo hopping a freight	211
A magazine drawing showing a hobo waving at people on passenger train	212
Carolyn Jody & family at Mount Rushmore	212
A hometown bakery	213
A young and apparently lucky Rod Nelson	213
A 1935 Chevrolet Standard two door	214
The camp bus	214
Swim time	215
Camps sign post	215
Northwestern Bank Weather Ball atop bank building	216
Vapor lock struck again	217
Pen knife	218
Dick Myslajek asks "Where did we go last summer?"	218
Jean Torgerson and her dad out fishing	219
Northwest Orient Airlines Statocrusier	219
The Larson Bros. Meat delivery truck	221
The Nuthouse	221
Checkers	221
Boy Scouts	222
St. Clements' first communion class	222
Prescott Glee Club from 1951 (from Sandy Cederstrom Rorem collection)	222
Sheridan 9th grade graduation – Bob Peters and friends (from Bob Peters collection)	222
Three unidentified kids in front of lake cabin	222
Map locating Nordeast area schools	223
A 1936 Buick and an unidentified family	224
Larry Kohout	224
Larry Kohout (holding brother Jack) and brother Dick	225
A block of Johnson Street stores (first one now occupied by the Que Viet Village House Restaurant)	226
Larry Kohout with friends from a family social organization	226
Carolyn Jody (from the Carolyn Jody Hagford collection)	226
A long gone school, possibly Holland – write if you recognize it	227
Another first communion class – unidentified	227
A Central Avenue liquor store	228
Northeast Christian Center Church	228
Boy on a baby scooter	228
Block Housing, like the Quonset huts, these were erected at the end of WWII to provide housing for the returning GIs	228
A Minnesota Territorial Centennial plate	228
A '40s or '50s era cash register	228

Title	Page
A hand pump for raising well water	229
A portion of the 1946 Prescott Kindergarten Class (from Sandy Cederstrom Rorem collection)	230
Candy counter at Lucy's	230
One of our many churches (D Myslajek drawing)	230
Three unidentified boys hamming it up in front of their fireplace	231
Mom setting up the television for three unidentified boys	231
Man on boarding ramp for a Douglas DC3 aircraft	231
Our Lady of Lourds church	231
Gloria Dei Lutheran church	232
One of the Nordeast houses built as you go up the "hill"	232
Joe Dimagio	232
Fidelity State Bank on Central Avenue	232
Grace Manor on Lowry Avenue	233
Three kids playing using scooter and trike	233
Sister Elizabeth Kenny gets a good bye kiss as she is leaving Minneapolis for her last time.	234
The 1946 March of Dimes poster child, Donald Anderson	234
The 1948 March of Dimes poster child Terry Tullos	235

Title	Page
Sister Elizabeth Kenny waves good bye before boarding her plane	235
The 1949 March of Dimes poster child Linda Brown	235
The 1950 March of Dimes poster child Wanda Wiley	236
The 1952 March of Dimes poster child Larry Jim Gross	236
Sister Kenny with one of the many volunteers	236
The ominous mushroom cloud	237
Unidentified children from the Quonset huts on 15th and Fillmore – Courtesy of the Minnesota Historical Society	237
A 10-year-old Louie Paff	238
A more modern Ritz Theater	238
Viewing Cross Lake through the trees	238
A vignette of the Grain Belt Brewing building	239
General Eisenhower appears before congress	239
One of the bigger houses built in Nordeast	239
Carolyn Jody (from the Carolyn Jody Hagford collection)	240
Holland School taken from the air (to belabor the obvious)	240
A vignette of moderate Nordeast houses	240
Larson kids and friend in a wagon (from the David Larson collection)	241

Title	Page
Nordeast homes down in the valley	241
One of the first McDonald's hamburger stands (15 cent hamburgers) in our area	242
Four-year-old Marilyn Sexton (from the Marilyn Sexton Lubrecht collection)	242
Paper shack – where news delivery boys got their papers	242
A snow fort	243
Old Nordeast Minneapolis residences	243
Polly and Penny Grivna (or the other way around) at Sheridan 9th grade graduation (from the Bob Peters collection)	243
Marilyn Sexton and her mother (from the Marilyn Sexton Lubrecht collection)	244
One of the park bandstands	244
Boy Scout camp	244
Van Cleve School	245
Jean Torgerson and her blue bike and an unidentified friend (from the Jean Torgerson Strong collection)	245
Sheridan Grade School/Junior High as shot down the alley from across Broadway	246
A still shot from Meet Me in Saint Lewis the senior class play of the Edison graduation class of 1958	246
One of the old neighborhood stores the stood on the island of land formed by Brighton Avenue NE and Cleveland Street	246

Title	Page
The State Theater in downtown Minneapolis	246
Sandy Cederstrom (from the Sandy Cederstrom Rorem collection)	247
A 1958 view of Hennepin Avenue at 2nd Street	247
A water pump from one of our parks	247
An unidentified woman in her garden	247
A beloved Schwinn Cruiser	248
The full Sheridan Band (from the Sharron Matt Weglinski collection)	248
The Nordeast is Beautiful button (from the Rod Nelson collection)	249